Bibliographic information published by the German National Library:

The German National Library lists this publication in the National Bibliography; detailed bibliographic data are available on the Internet at http://dnb.dnb.de .

Imprint:

Copyright © 2015 GRIN Verlag, Open Publishing GmbH
Print and binding: Books on Demand GmbH, Norderstedt Germany
ISBN: 9783668443822

This book at GRIN:

http://www.grin.com/en/e-book/365482/analysis-of-nuclear-transport-signals

Silvana Wolf

Analysis of Nuclear Transport Signals

GRIN Publishing

GRIN - Your knowledge has value

Since its foundation in 1998, GRIN has specialized in publishing academic texts by students, college teachers and other academics as e-book and printed book. The website www.grin.com is an ideal platform for presenting term papers, final papers, scientific essays, dissertations and specialist books.

Lehrstuhl für Bioinformatik und Computerbiologie

Rostlab

Bachelorarbeit

in Bioinformatik

Analysis of Nuclear Transport Signals

Silvana Wolf

Kurzzusammenfassung

Analyse nuklearer Transportsignale

Der nukleare Proteintransport ist ein grundlegender Mechanismus der Zelle, welcher einer Reihe biologischer Prozesse vorhergeht. Der klassische Transport für nukleare Proteine erfolgt durch sogenannte Karyopherine, welche die Proteine ein und aus dem Nukleus schleusen. Im Feld des nuklearen Proteintransports sind drei Haupttypen von Signalen für den nuklearen Import (NLS) bekannt: monopartite, bipartite und PY-NLS. Studien zum nuklearen-export Signalen (NES) fokussieren den speziellen Typ Leucin reicher Signale.

Das erste Ziel dieser Studie war es NLSdb auf den aktuellen Stand der Forschung zu bringen. NLSdb ist eine Datenbank für nukleare-lokalisations-Signale und enthält eine Sammlung von 114 experimentellen und 196 potentiellen Import-Signalen. Ein Set von 2452 neuen Signalen mit publiziertem experimentellem Nachweis aus der Literatur wurde als Entwicklungsset genutzt. Ein *in silico* Mutagenese-Ansatz wurde auf diesem Entwicklungsset angewandt. Dies führte zu 4301 neuen potentiellen NLSs, welche in nuklearen Proteinen gefunden wurden.

Zusätzlich zur Datensammlung wurden durch Protein Sequenz Analyse die Eigenschaften (Funktion, Ort und Vorkommen) der Signale und der durch sie transportierten Proteine untersucht. Die genaue Betrachtung der Signaleigenschaften erlaubt eine mögliche Untergruppierung und genauere Angabe von Sequenzmustern der verschiedenen Signaltypen. Verschiedene Tests wurden gemacht um die genutzten Daten zu bewerten. Sie zeigen, dass das Update die alte Version von NLSdb verbessert und heben die Nützlichkeit der Vorhersagemöglichkeit von neuen Signalen hervor.

Die Ergebnisse dieser Studie reflektieren den Fortschritt in der Wissenschaft, bringen weiteres Wissen im Bereich des nuklearen Transports und betonen den Nutzen der Bioinformatik für die Entdeckung neuer Erkenntnisse in der Biologie. Nuklearer Proteintransport tritt in vielen interessanten Forschungsbereichen auf, zum Beispiel bei Allergien, Krebs oder anderen Erkrankungen. Die Ergebnisse dieser Arbeit bieten eine gute Ausgangslage für weitere Forschungsarbeiten.

Abstract

Analysis of Nuclear Transport Signal

Nuclear transport of proteins is a basic cellular mechanism preceding a lot of biological processes. The classical transport mechanism for nuclear proteins involves karyopherins importing and exporting the proteins. The karyopherins recognize typically nuclear transport signals in the protein sequence. Three main types of nuclear localization signals (NLS) are focused in the scientific field of nuclear protein transport: monopartite, bipartite and PY-NLS. In studies on nuclear export signals (NES) the specific type of leucine-rich signals is often investigated.

The first goal of this thesis was to update NLSdb, a database containing 114 experimental and 194 potential NLS, to the current state of available data. Towards this end, a set of 2452 novel signals with published experimental evidence was extracted from the literature and used as development set. An *in silico* mutagenesis approach was applied to this set to detect 4301 novel potential NLS in nuclear proteins. We matched these potential NLS in protein sequences of unannotated subcellular localization to identify nuclear proteins. We were able to confirm the predicted localization using our potential NLS in literature.

Additional to the collection of data, an extensive analysis on protein sequences containing NLS and NES was performed to provide insights into subcellular localization of proteins and their occurrence in various organisms. A clustering of sequences of NLS led to the separation of signals into distinct sub-groups with a clear definition of a consensus sequence for each sub-group. Aligning potential NLS against the sub-groups resulted in a refinement of the consensus sequences.

The results from this study reflect the scientific progress, lead to further knowledge in the field of nuclear transport and highlight the usability of bioinformatics methods for the discovery of new insights in biology. Nuclear transport is related to many interesting researches, for example allergic reactions, cancer and other diseases. The outcome of this work provides a good fundament for other studies with nuclear transport signals.

0.   Abstract

Table of Contents

1. Introduction

1.1. Cellular compartmentalization

The analysis of nuclear transport signals opens up a biological field that is based on fundamental processes within the cells functionality. Every eukaryotic cell is divided into compartments. The compartmentalization through the cellular organelles forms physical barriers building up special areas with best circumstances for biological processes and molecular functions [Verkman2002]. The nucleus is one of the organelles. It is, like many of them, enclosed by an own membrane and different layers. The nucleus itself is divided into sub-compartments. Similar to the membranes of cellular compartments, the outer nuclear sub-compartment called nuclear envelope constitutes a barrier for all molecules excessing the diffusion size. It is build up by two nuclear membranes. The outer membrane is connected with the endoplasmic reticulum and the inner membrane interacts with the nuclear lamina. Nuclear pore complexes (NPCs) are the gates for molecules, bigger than diffusion size (<= 40-65kDa), to pass the nuclear envelope [Cautain2014].

In this study, the molecules of interest, traveling in and out of the nucleus, were proteins. Once a protein is transcribed in the cell's nucleus, exported and translated in the cell's cytoplasm and then folded into its final shape, it can be moved to its functional destination. For some proteins this destination is the nucleus and the protein's sequence carries special nuclear localization signals for the transport into it.

1.2. Nuclear localization signal (NLS)

There are many ways of transporting a protein into the nucleus [Wagstaff2009]. One of the nuclear import mechanisms, which is called the classical nuclear import mechanism, depends on specific nuclear localization signals that are recognized by the so-called karyopherins importing the proteins through the NPCs. The transporter proteins are called importin-α and importin-β. In the classical pathway the signal is bound by the binding pockets of the importin-α. Importin-β binds to that complex and functions as target for the NPCs. After passing the nuclear pore complex, a protein called Ran GTPase, binds to the importin-β and the hydrolysis to GDP brings the complex to release the NLS containing protein [Curmi2010]. In this study the focus lies on three main types of signals: monopartite, bipartite and PY-NLS. The first two signals follow mainly the import mechanism of the classical pathway. The PY-NLSs are transported into the nucleus by the karyopherin-β2 pathway [Lange2008].

1.2.1. Monopartite NLS

The first and most investigated NLS is the monopartite signal. It was first described as a nuclear import signal in the simian virus 40 by Colledge et al. [Colledge1986]. From 1986 on, the signal still keeps attention in the field of nuclear localization signals. Monopartite NLSs are short signals, containing 4-10 amino acids, which are mostly basic. The consensus sequence for the most conserved part of this pattern is K-(K/R)-X-(K/R) [Leung2003].

1.2.2. Bipartite NLS

The bipartite signals can be described as two stretches of monopartite signals (two basic stretches), combined by a 10-12 amino acids long linker sequence in the middle. It is still not completely resolved how this signal sequence looks and what the functional areas are. In literature putative consensus sequences for the bipartite signal are described as the following: $(K/R)(K/R)X_{10-12}K(K/R)(K/R)$ and $(K/R)(K/R)X_{10-12}K(K/R)X(K/R)$ [Kosugi2008]. In addition, examples showing the activity and influence of the linker part have been discovered [Kosugi2008].

1.2.3. PY-NLS

A more recently observed signal is the PY-NLS. As mentioned above the proteins with these signals are imported through the karyopherin-β2 pathway. Other than classical signals the PY-NLS can be directly bound by the karyopherin-β2, which was first described in 2006 [Lee2006]. The signals have both a strongly conserved C-terminal region and a long and variable region at the signal's N-terminus. The C-terminal end of this pattern most of the time is indicated as $(R/H/K)X_{2-5}PY$, with the characteristic of a proline followed by a tyrosine. A division of types of PY-signals can be made, depending on the N-terminal amino acids. Regarding to this part of the PY-signals, they can be classified as hydrophobic or basic [Süel2008]. Two consensus sequences are defined for the two types of the PY-NLS: $(LIMHFYVPQ)-(GAS)-(LIMHFYVPRQK)-(LIMHFYVPRQK)-X_{7-12}-(RKH)-X_{2-5}PY$ for hydrophobic PY-NLSs and $(KR)-X_{0-2}-(KR)-(KR)-X_{3-10}-(RKH)-X_{1-5}PY$ for basic PY-NLSs [Lange2008]. According to this two classifications of PY-NLSs the expected length of the signals varies between 16-24 amino acids in hydrophobic PY-NLSs and 11-23 residues in basic PY-NLSs.

1.3. Nuclear export signal (NES)

Some proteins also need to be exported out of the nucleus for further functions in the cell's interior. For this purpose, their sequences carry nuclear export signals. The scientific research on NESs started as early as the research on NLSs. First described was the nuclear export signal in HIV-1 [Fischer1995]. Later, a focus on NESs came along with the publications about investigation of PY-NLS. The best described type of nuclear export signals is the leucine rich NES, but the definition of a consensus sequence leads to the conflict of matching random regions in the sequence [Dong2009]. Similar to the nuclear import sequences, the export sequences can be classified into more conserved groups of NESs [Kosugi3.2008]. The common pathway for nuclear export is the CRM1-depend pathway [Fornerod1997]. CRM1 belongs to the protein family of importin-β and acts as exportin protein. Similar to the classical import pathway, the export protein binds Ran GTPase and then binds at the NES of the cargo protein. The complex is then able to exit the nucleus [Kosugi2.2008].

1.4. NLSdb - Database of nuclear localization signals 1.0

The starting point for this thesis was NLSdb1.0, the database of nuclear localization signals, containing 114 literature curated experimentally verified NLSs and 194 potential NLSs found through iterated 'in silico mutagenesis' [Nair2003]. It was published in 2003 and is still a highly referenced and used database. NLSdb1.0 is a reliable source for finding NLSs, but the earlier mentioned developments and discoveries of signals types, indicate that an update of the database is necessary.

1.5. Motivation

To understand the impact of this investigated cellular mechanism, a short look on the function of proteins entering the nucleus can be taken. Nuclear proteins can be affecting the regulation of the gene expression. Regarding to this, nuclear import of proteins is basically involved in everything related to DNA regulation. For example, allergic reactions, coming from an overexpression of inflammation, involve cytokine proteins. Cytokines can be traced back to an imported protein changing specifically the DNA replication rate [Aggarwal2014].

Following this importance for basic knowledge of nuclear transport signals the main goals of this Bachelor thesis were twofold:

First, it was aimed to update the first version of NLSdb. NLSdb1.0 is a reliable source for finding NLSs and their proteins. The database provided 114 experimentally verified and 195 computationally predicted potential NLSs. However, the last update was performed in 2003. Much new research was done in the area of NLSs/NESs and the database did not distinguish between different types of NLSs/NESs. Thus we performed the necessary update of NLSdb1.0 to the current state of available signal data.

Secondly, various protein sequence analyses were performed on the dataset of 2452 novel experimental and 4301 potential NLSs and their proteins to provide insights into their biology. Therefore we inquired several questions:

- Do homologous protein sequences have similar signals?
- From which organism are the proteins with known nuclear localization signals?
- What are the subcellular location annotations of proteins containing NLSs?
- Can we predict subcellular location using the potential signals?
- Can we define sub-groups within the signal types and refine consensus sequences for the different groups of signals?

This all together with the new potential signals can lead to a more comprehensive understanding of one of the cell's basic mechanisms that affects cells activity in many ways. It can also be used as foundation for many further studies.

2. Materials and Methods

2.1. Data collection of experimentally verified nuclear transport signals

NLSdb1.0 was released in 2003 [Nair2003]. Experimental NLSs and NESs were collected from literature and databases published after 2003 to update NLSdb1.0.

Different keywords were used for the search of publications listing experimental NLSs: "importin binging signals", "*In vitro* NLS", "nuclear localization", "nuclear localization signal datasets", "nuclear localization signals review", "bipartite NLS", "PY-NLS", "signal peptides nuclear import" and "signals for nuclear transport". For finding NESs the keyword "nuclear export signals" was used. Additionally to provide lists of experimentally verified NLSs and NESs, the listed sources gave a good overview of the biological background of nuclear transport signals, the most recent and usable NLSs containing databases and computational tools for signal prediction. Especially, the publication of Marfori *et al.* provided this [Marfori2011].

To accept publications as reliable source, the signals needed to be experimentally verified. Our definition of a reliable evidence was conform to the definition of the experimentally verified signals curated for NLSdb1.0 : "Our main criteria for 'accepting' NLSs were that the signal was proven sufficient to mediate the nuclear transport of a non-nuclear protein to the nucleus and that deleting the NLS prevented the nuclear import." [Nair2003].

Additional to the literature curation, proteins and signals were extracted from Swiss-Prot entries [Swiss-Prot2004] containing an experimentally annotated NLS. Compared to the other sources for NLSs, Swiss-Prot was incomplete in the annotation of nuclear proteins and their NLSs. Some of the experimentally verified proteins from publications were sorted into Trembl instead of Swiss-Prot and some nuclear localization annotation and NLSs proved in literature were missing in Swiss-Prot. For this reason, Uniprot [UniProt2015] was the database used for extracting annotations and accession numbers (ACs) for proteins coming from all sources.

2.1.1. NLSs

The sources that were used for the collection of nuclear localization signals are given below. From each source the signals and the Uniprot-ACs for the proteins carrying the signals, as well as information (about organism, location annotation and GO terms), were extracted. Table 1 shows the sources and the number of experimentally verified signals that could be found in them.

Database	NLSdb1.0 [Nair2003]	Lange [Lange2008]	SeqNLS [Lin2013]	Swiss-Prot [Bairoch2004]	PY-NLS Sources [Lee2006] [Süel2008]
Number of signals	114	104	122	2243	19

Table 1: Number of experimental NLSs extracted from the different sources. The signal extraction procedure is described in sections 2.1.1.1.-2.1.1.6

2.1.1.1.   The database NLSdb1.0

As mentioned in 1.4., NLSdb1.0 is database containing 114 experimentally validated and 196 potential NLSs [Nair2003]. The 114 experimentally verified signals were collected by searching the literature. The 194 potential NLSs were created by an iterated *in silico* mutagenesis approach. In the first algorithm step, at every position in the sequence of the experimental signals the amino acids were mutated to another amino acid or were removed. The mutated signals were then tested to match exclusively a dataset containing nuclear proteins. Since it´s publication in 2003, NLSdb1.0 was cited each year on average 10 times (Figure 1). Monthly, its webserver was being accessed by about 100 unique IP addresses. NLSdb1.0 listed for each signal the Uniprot [UniProt2015] ID of the protein that carries the signal.

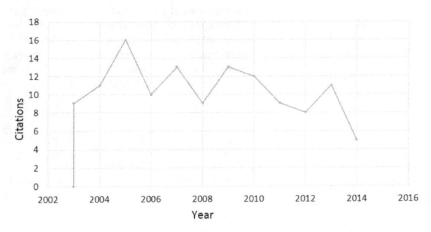

Figure 1: Yearly citation of NLSdb [Nair2003] paper since it´s publication in 2003 from Goolge.analytics.dom.

2.1.1.2.   Publication of Lange *et al.*

The publication of Lange *et al.* [Lange2008] provided monopartite and bipartite NLSs potentially imported via the classical pathway with importin-α [Lange2007]. In their study, the prediction tool PSORT 2 [Nakai1999] was used to find classical monopartite and bipartite signals in the yeast proteome found in GenBank [Benson2013]. The predicted proteins were tested *in vivo* to get an experimental evidence for them. To prove the nuclear localization of proteins containing such a NLS, a GFP-fusion screening was made. All proteins using the classical pathway of nuclear import interact with importin-α [Curmi2010]. To find this interactions, the proteins of interest were looked up on the interaction database BioGRID [Aryamontri2015]. Only those signals having both a nuclear localization and an interaction with importin-α were used for this study. After filtering the data following these restrictions, 68 yeast proteins with multiple signals were left. In these proteins, 70 unique monopartite and 35 unique bipartite NLSs were listed.

2.1.1.3.   Prediction tool SeqNLS

SeqNLS is a tool for prediction of NLS using pattern matching and a scoring scheme [Lin2013]. The tool was trained on the experimental signals of NLSdb1.0. Their test dataset was compiled from two subsets:
First, the yeast dataset of 43 proteins with 51 experimentally verified signals collected from literature by NLStradamus (another tool for NLS prediction based on Hidden Markov Models) [Ba2009].
Secondly, a hybrid dataset, containing 57 proteins from different organism with 72 annotated NLSs curated from literature, published after 2010.
All together 122 unique signals and 93 unique Uniprot-ACs were collected from SeqNLS.

2.1.1.4.   The Swiss-Prot database

The source with the highest count of proteins used for this project was the Swiss-Prot database [Bairoch2004]. The information on the presence of a nuclear localization signal (location in the sequence, type of signal and evidence) in a protein were provided in the Motif" or "Region" section of the "Family and Domain" annotation of it´s Swiss-Prot entry. The "Motif" and "Region" sections were screened for the following keywords for a signal to be included into our dataset:

- Nuclear localization signal
- Bipartite nuclear localization signal
- Nuclear import signal

Note, that during later stages of the work we discovered the following additional keywords for nuclear localization signals that were not included into our dataset:

- Unconventional nuclear localization signal
- Required for nuclear localization
- Required (and sufficient) for nuclear import
- Sufficient for nuclear import
- Required for nucleolar localization

Note, the annotations of NLSs in the "Motif" and "Region" section refer to the same. Personal communication with the Uniprot consortium revealed the NLSs within the "Region" section as annotation errors intended to be included in the "Motif" section.

Additional criteria for a nuclear localization signals to be included was the evidence of its annotation. The evidences were given by "Evidence Codes Ontology" [Chibucos2014], short ECOs.

These annotations were classified into manual or automatic assertions. Manual assertions were given by the four following ECOs:

- "ECO:0000269", manually curated information with published experimental evidence.
- "ECO:0000250", manually curated information propagated from a related experimentally characterized protein.
- "ECO:0000255" manual assertions for information generated by the UniProtKB automatic annotation system (e.g. with Prosite-Rule [Sigrist2010] as source). This was also used for information generated by various sequence analysis programs used during the manual curation process verified by a curator.
- "ECO:0000305", manually curated information inferred by a curator based on his/her scientific knowledge or on the scientific content of an article.

In total 3874 unique protein sequences with 2243 unique signals in either "Motif" or "Region" section were extracted from Swiss-Prot.

2.1.1.5.   PY-NLS sources

Two publications were used as sources for PY-NLSs. The first source was published in 2006 by Lee et al. [Lee2006]. They focused on signals transported by the karyopherin-β2 pathway and defined the sequence of PY-NLSs as having an "overall basic character, and possess a central hydrophobic or basic motif followed by a C-terminal R/H/KX2–5PY consensus sequence" [Lee2006]. They provided 7 already known experimental NLSs and proved some of their 81 predicted PY-NLSs to be functional NLSs [Lee2006]. We extracted 9 signals with experimental evidence from this publication.

The other source was the publication of Süel et al. from 2008 [Süel2008] that collect experimentally validated and computationally predicted PY-NLSs. They used these signals to prove their functionality as nuclear import signals in different in vivo and in vitro methods. Only the signals with a very reliable evidence were taken as data for this study [Süel2008]. We extracted 10 PY-NLSs with in vivo and in vitro evidence from this list.

Most of the signal sequences were listed in form of consensus sequences provided together with the signals´ position in the protein sequence. To have comparable data the signals were extracted according to their position in the protein sequence. This resulted in 19 unique signals in 17 unique proteins.

2.1.1.6.   Others

Some other sources were discovered in the process of literature search for signals. They were not directly used, but were informative and should be mentioned in order to provide information for further studies.

The nuclear protein database (NPD) [Bickmore2002] is a well-structured database of known nuclear proteins from vertebrates. It is possible to search the database by sequence motifs, including monopartite NLSs. The results showed the start and stop position of the signals, but they did not tell what the evidence of this signals is. NPD listed 1443 proteins with a monopartite NLS.

Another source for knowledge of differences in the sequences of NLSs, was the work of Kosugi *et al.* [Kosugi2008]. By an *in vitro* NLSs screening in random peptide libraries they provided about 500 sequences containing monopartite NLSs. Additionally, a mutational sequence analysis resulted in artificial NLSs experimentally verified by an *in vivo* approach. A consensus sequence tend to be either too general matching random sequences or too specific missing putative NLSs [Kosugi2008]. Doing their study, Kosugi *et al.* characterized six different groups of nuclear localizations signals imported through the classical pathway and provided consensus sequences for each of them (Table 2). The classification resolved the problem arising by a single consensus sequences. Additionally, the binding position at importin-α for each of the signal type was discovered. Another observation from their study was the regulative activity of the linker region in bipartite signal [Kosugi2008].

NLS class	Consensus sequence[a]
Class 1	KR(K/R)R, K(K/R)RK
Class 2	(P/R)XXKR($^\cdot$DE)(K/R)
Class 3	KRX(W/F/Y)XXAF
Class 4	(R/P)XXKR(K/R)($^\cdot$DE)
Class 5	LGKR(K/R)(W/F/Y)
Bipartite	KRX_{10-12}K(KR)(KR)[b]
	KRX_{10-12}K(KR)X(K/R)[b]

Table 2: Consensus sequences of six classes of importin-α -dependent NLSs taken from Kosugi *et al.* [Kosugi2008]

2.1.2. NESs

Five sources for collecting nuclear export signals were used. Table 3 lists the number of protein sequences with a NES found in each of the sources. Only the column for NESMapper shows the number of signals.

Database	ValidNESs [Fu2012]	NESdb [Xu2012]	NESbase [Cour2003]	Swiss-Prot [Bairoch2004]	NESMapper [Kosugi2014]
Number of proteins	221	175	75	971	343

Table 3: Number of NESs extracted from the different sources

These sources focus on NESs exported via the classical pathway mediated by karyopherin-β2 and mostly contained leucine-rich NESs.

2.1.2.1.   The database ValidNESs

The database ValidNESs contained 262 leucine-rich nuclear export signals in 221 protein sequences curated from literature [Fu2012]. They also provided NESsential, a tool for predicting nuclear export signals based on sequence structure, disordered and solvent accessibility [Fu2011].

2.1.2.2.   The NESdb

Another database for NESs was NESdb [Xu2012]. NESdb listed 175 proteins containing a NES with experimental evidence and published reference. Besides, NESdb provided 196 proteins with putative NESs, which were not yet proven to be functional sequences. This work was published in 2012 and was another recent source for finding nuclear proteins and NLSs online. Altogether we extracted the signals of the 175 unique proteins.

2.1.2.3.   The NESbase database

The third database specialized on nuclear export signals was NESbase [Cour2003]. Published in 2003 this was the first work on NESs and they were pioneers of NES research. The signals listed in this database, were also manually curated from literature and show a leucine-rich motif. The database contained 75 proteins with one or more NESs, as well as information about necessity and sufficiency for nuclear protein transport mediated by the signals [Cour2003].

2.1.2.4.   The Swiss-Prot database

Similar to the description in 2.1.1.4., NESs were searches in Swiss-Prot database [Bairoch2004]. The key words for nuclear export signals in the "Motif" and "Region" section were:

- Nuclear export signal
- nuclear export sequence.

Two additional keywords for nuclear export signals were discovered in a later state of work:

- required (and sufficient) for nuclear export
- Sufficient for nuclear export.

The evidence codes were the same as in 2.1.1.4. In total 971 proteins containing 433 NESs were extracted from Swiss-Prot "Motif" and "Region" section.

2.1.2.5.   The prediction tool NESMapper

The last source in Table 3 for NESs was NESMapper. NESMapper is another prediction tool for finding leucine-rich NESs [Kosugi2014]. The prediction algorithm was based on profiles created by a scoring of activity-affecting residues in the signal sequence. They used datasets from three different sources for NESMapper development:

- First, 205 NESs from ValidNESs
- Second, 32 signals from DUB NES (signals of the human deubiquitinases protein family[Santisteban2012]

- Third, 311 artificial NESs from their own study.

Similar to their study, described in 2.1.1.6., they used signals screening in random peptide libraries and applied a mutational approach to create 311 artificial signals. The functionality of some of the artificial NLSs was proven *in vivo*. All together this source listed 343 experimentally verified nuclear export signals.

2.1.2.6. Other

Similar to 2.1.1.6., the nuclear protein database (NPD) [Bickmore2002] can be listed as an additional source, which was not included in the current datasets, because of time limits. The NPD listed 297 proteins containing a NES.

2.1.3. Test set – unannotated Swiss-Prot proteins

All eukaryotic proteins without a subcellular location annotation were collected from Swiss-Prot. This set was redundancy reduced by Uniqueprot [Mika2003] and then tested once with the signals of NLSdb1.0 and once with NLSdb2.0 for benchmarking these two versions.

NLSdb1.0 is based on eukaryotic organism. They used human, mouse, fly, worm, yeast and cress. NLSdb2.0 used all organism found to have a NLS out of Uniprot, so a comparison based on eukaryotic proteins was suitable for both versions.

2.2. *In silico* mutagenesis

The previous described signals and sources were all for collecting an experimentally verified set of NLSs. For an update of NLSdb1.0 potential signals were also needed. These potential signals were created by a mutagenesis approach similar to the approach of NLSdb1.0 [Nair2003].

2.2.1. Sets of nuclear and non-nuclear proteins

Before the mutated signals could be used, sets for matching them, were needed. A nuclear and a non-nuclear protein set were created out of proteins annotated in Swiss-Prot. The decision whether a protein was included in one of the sets was based on the subcellular location annotation in Swissprot files. In section 2.1.1.4. about Swiss-Prot, the different ECOs and their meaning were specified. Besides these ECOs, a location annotation without such an evidence code also stand for a reliable source. On the Uniprot web page for evidences [Evidence2014] it was explained, that not all annotations were yet ordered into the ECO system, but annotations without any code still mean there is evidence for them. A protein was sorted into the nuclear set if it had a nuclear or chromosome related subcellular annotation with either "ECO:0000269" (manually curated information with published experimental evidence) or just the text without an evidence code. For the non-nuclear dataset the same restrictions in terms of ECOs were set. Every protein with an annotation that differs from "nucleus" or "chromosome" was sorted into the non-nuclear set.

2.2.2. Mutagenesis approach

The development set of 2452 experimentally verified NLSs was used as training set for the iterative *in silico* mutagenesis approach. The algorithm was divided into three main steps:

Firstly, the size of the development set was decreased for keeping only experimental NLSs that can be found in proteins with annotated nuclear location in Swiss-Prot. Only the signals that did not occur in protein sequences of the non-nuclear set were taken. These signals were then tested to occur in the protein sequences of the nuclear dataset.

Secondly, we performed a mutational step, using the signals of the reduced development set as input. Figure 2 visualizes the *in silico* mutation with an example. Every signal was mutated at each position into all 20 amino acids. All possible mutations of every signal were tested again for their occurrence in the protein sequences of the non-nuclear and the nuclear dataset.

The last step was an iteration on the mutated signals. Only mutated signals matching in the nuclear proteins, but not in the non-nuclear proteins, were sorted into the result set and shortened by one position at the end of the signals. The shorter signals still matching exclusively in the sequences of the nuclear protein set were further shortened. This was repeated until the created sequence matches either in none or both of the two protein sets. All resulting signals formed the set of potential NLSs.

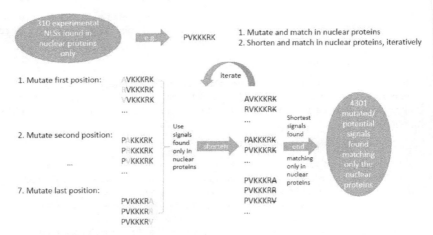

Figure 2: *In silico* mutagenesis approach. First, a mutation at every position in the initial NLS into all 20 amino acids was done. Secondly, the mutated signals matching exclusively in the nuclear protein sequences, were shortened at their last position. The shortened signals were tested again to match only in the nuclear protein set. The matching signals are iteratively shortened until they did not match in the nuclear set, or matched in the nuclear and in the non-nuclear protein set. All mutated and shortened signals found to match the nuclear set only, were used included in a set of potential NLSs.

The fact that the signals were first mutated and then iteratively shortened led to the appearance of supersets within the list of potential signals. A superset was defined as every set of potential signals containing another potential signal (see Table 4). Not all potential signals had supersets. Anyway, to bypass these supersets only the shortest signals of each superset were kept.

Experimental signal	KRRRQKIRKYTMRR
Potential sequences in superset	KRRRQKIRKYTMR
	KRRRQKIRKYTM
	KRRRQKIRKYT
	KRRRQKIRKY
	KRRRQKIRK
	KRRRQKIR
	KRRRQKI
Final potential signal	KRRRQK

Table 4: Example superset of potential signals. The experimental signal from the development dataset was mutated. All potential signals (the ones in the superset and the final signal) were matched only in protein sequences of nuclear proteins. We kept only the shortest potential signal for the final dataset of potential signals.

2.3.   Data analyses

Due to time limits, all work described here was based on NLSs only.

2.3.1.   Data pre-processing tools

Blast

Blast is the standard program for sequence comparison based on local alignments. We compared the similarity of the protein sequences with blast to infer the homology of the proteins from our datasets. The algorithm finds sequences in a database either identical or similar to a sequence searched [Altschul1990]. For our purpose the version PSI-Blast was used. In PSI-Blast the search is iteratively based on position-specific scoring matrices (PSSM). We chose an e-value lower than 0.001 and 2 iterations as appropriate parameters for significant alignments.

Cd-hit

Cd-hit is a tool we used for redundancy reduction of sequences [Li2001]. Cd-hit sorts the sequences by their length. The longest sequence is the representative for the cluster and other sequences are compared by sequence similarity to the representative sequence and sorted into its cluster if the similarity is above a given threshold. If the similarity is lower, the compared sequence is being set to be the representative for a new cluster. In this way, a very fast grouping of all sequences is achieved. Short words from 2 to 5 letters are compared between two sequences, representing high identity segments. The number of these short words corresponds to the sequence identity. Therefore, only proteins with a number of identical short words higher than a threshold are aligned to speed up the algorithm.

We used Cd-hit on the sequences of proteins containing NLSs to identify sets of sequence similarity of 100%, 80%, 60% and 40% (c = 1.0, 0.8, 0.6, 0.4, respectively). We chose a word length of 5 (n=5) for 100% and 80% and of 4 (n=4) for 60% and 40%. We matched the experimental NLSs to the sequences of the redundancy reduced sets to see if proteins with homolog sequences have similar proteins.

Uniqueprot

Cd-hit is limited to a minimum of 40% sequence identity. Therefore, we used Uniqueprot, (another tool for redundancy reduction of protein sequences [Mika2003]) to compute protein sets with 20% sequence identify and to find the signals occurring in this set. The algorithms of Uniqueprot and Cd-hit differ. Uniqueprot uses Blast for aligning the sequences. A similarity score between each pair of sequences, called HSSP value or HVAL (see Formula below) is calculated based on the blast alignment [Sander1991] [Rost1999]. Proteins sharing the same HVAL higher than a threshold (t), in our case t = 0, are grouped. For all groups a greedy algorithm keeps one protein and removes the other. After this, the HVAL between all remaining proteins is lower than the threshold and the sequence similarity reduced. If the threshold for the HVAL is 0, it corresponds to a sequence similarity of maximum 20 % for the sequences having more than 450 residues aligned.

$$= \mathrm{PID} - \begin{cases} 100 & \text{for } L \leq 11 \\ 480 \cdot L^{-0.32 \cdot (1 + \exp(-L/1000))} & \text{for } L \leq 450 \\ 19.5 & \text{for } L > 450 \end{cases}$$

Formula: HSSP value formula, where PID = the number of identical residues in the alignment, calculated by blast*100 − L and L = length of the alignment (without gaps).

We applied the formula for the HSSP value on the alignment results from Blast. We investigated the distribution of similar protein sequences containing NLSs using the calculated HVALs to infer the homology of proteins carrying a NLS.

Clustering approach from Mikael Bodén's lab at Queensland University

To identify unique groups within the sets of each type of NLSs, the signal sequences were clustered using an approach developed by Mikael Bodén's lab at the University of Queensland. The advantage of this method over other clustering approaches is the ability to process a large amount of sequences (> 4000 sequences). Working with sequence motifs always asks for a consensus rule, for this reason the clustering and grouping of the types of NLSs was used for refining consensus sequences.

We performed pairwise alignment of all the NLSs sequences for each signal type to calculate the most likely evolutionary distances - in the form of a distance matrix - between them. We used these distances to construct a phylogenetic tree for each type of NLSs by the hierarchical clustering method UPGMA (unweighted pair-group method using arithmetic averages) [Sneath1973]. We could identify distinct sub-groups of NLSs from the phylogenetic trees inspired by a large scale clustering approach developed by Krause *et al* [Krause2005]. Consensus patterns in the form of position-weight-matrices (PWMs) were derived for the sub-groups. We visualized these consensus sequences as sequence logos. We scored alignments of the set of potential NLSs against the PWMs of the monopartite sub-groups. To find the most similar sub-groups for each potential NLS, we ranked the PWM match scores for potential sequences against those of a background composed of 10000 completely random sequences. The monopartite signals in high ranking groups were aligned with all the best matching potential sequences with Clustal Omega [Sievers2011]. We visualized these alignments through the creation of additional sequence logos using

Weblogo [Crooks2004]. This allowed us to extend and refine the consensus sequences for each sub-group of monopartite NLSs.

A detailed explanation of the formulas and methods used in the clustering approach can be found in the supplementary material (on the DVD) – provided by Julian Zaugg, a PhD student in the group of Mikael Bodén.

2.3.2. Protein function and NLS prediction tools

PredictProtein

PredictProtein [Yachdav2014] is, as the name infers, a collection of prediction tool for structural and functional protein properties. We were interested in the subcellular location of proteins, where Swiss-Prot lacks an annotation. Loctree3 [Goldberg2014], a prediction tool for subcellular locations [Nair2005], was used to predict the location annotations of proteins.

PredictNLS

PredictNLS [Cokol2000] is a tool that searches the signals of NLSdb1.0 in a query sequence. The output file contains a list of the signals found in the sequence together with the signals' position. Additionally, it provides the information on whether the protein binds the DNA or not. PredictNLS was used to compare the signals from this study to NLSdb1.0.

3. Results and Discussion

The data from all sources were extracted and separated in three set for: monopartite, bipartite and PY-NLSs, respectively. The according UniprotKB-IDs and gene names of proteins with NLSs were mapped to Uniprot-ACs for further analyses.

3.1. Experimental development dataset

Sources	NLSdb1.0 (114NLSs)	Lange (105NLSs)	SeqNLS (122NLSs)	Swiss-Prot (2243NLSs)	PY-NLS (19NLSs)	All sources (2603NLSs)
Overlap						
NLSdb1.0		0	0	48	0	
Lange			6	16	0	
SeqNLS				19	0	
Swiss-Prot					0	
PY-NLS						
Additional to NLSdb1.0						2452

Table 5: Comparison of experimental NLSs from different sources. Combining the signals of all sources we got 2603 NLSs. Between the sources some of the signals overlapped. From the signals of NLSdb1.0 48 NLSs were found in the data collected from Swiss-Prot. The NLSs from Lange *et al.* and SeqNLS overlapped in 6 NLSs and had both an overlap with the signals extracted from Swiss-Prot, of 16 and 19 signals, respectively. The field "Additional to NLSdb1.0" lists 2452 unique signals collected in this study. This number is the number of all signals without the signals of NLSdb1.0 and without the overlapping signals between all sources (in total 37 unique signals overlapped).

Table 5 lists the number of NLSs extracted from each source and the overlap of signals between the sources. To find the overlap a simple sequence comparison was done. On the right side the column "All unique signal" shows the number of 2603 signals extracted from all sources. The row "Additional to NLSdb1.0" shows that 2452 new experimental signals were collected in this study. The first comparison row shows, that the signals in NLSdb1.0 had no overlap with the signals from Lange *et al.* or Lin *et al.* Furthermore only 48 signals of NLSdb1.0 were in the dataset collected from Swiss-Prot. A closer check for the 114 signals and their proteins validated that the proteins in NLSdb1.0 had a published evidence for their NLSs,s but yet no signal annotation in Swiss-Prot. The other two published sources also had a low overlap of 6 NLSs between their experimentally verified signals. Both overlapped with the signals extracted from the Swiss-Prot motif annotations: 16 signals from Lange *et al.* and 19 signals from SeqNLS were included in the Swiss-Prot data. Some of the 6 signals overlapping in the data from SeqNLS and Lange *et al.* also overlapped with the signals from Swiss-Prot. In total the number of unique overlapping signals is 37 (without considering the signal of NLSdb1.0). The "Additional to NLSdb1.0" lists the unique signals found additional to the signals of NLSdb1.0. On the first gaze the collection of new signals was an increase of data over more than 20 fold compared to the data of NLSdb1.0. The further results of analyses steps shed light on the quality of the new signals. It should be mentioned that consensus patterns were within the 114 signals of NLSdb1.0. Those did not match in a simple string comparison, therefore they were manually compared to the other signals. None of the manually compared signals was found in the datasets from other sources.

Table A1 in the appendix, shows the comparison of Uniprot-ACs of proteins carrying the experimental signals. In a comparison of proteins, it could also be seen, that Swiss-Prot had not included all experimental verified proteins found in literature. The initial collected NLSs from NLSdb1.0 and the proteins containing them, were still not correctly annotated in Swiss-Prot and had only a small overlap.

3.2. Properties of nuclear localization signals and their proteins

3.2.1. Sequence length

The distribution of the signal length mirrored the classification of the signal types (Sections1.2.1.-1.2.3.). A comparison of the length distributions of all types of NLSs is shown in Figure 3. Most of the monopartite signals (blue line) were distributed between lengths of 4 to 10 amino acids. The second peak of the blue line within a length of 16 to 18 amino acids corresponds to the peaks of bipartite (yellow line) and PY-NLSs (green line). As the number of signals of this two groups was much lower than the number of monopartite signals, this peaks possibly are the characteristic peaks of bipartite and PY-NLSs. This implies possible annotation errors for monopartite signals in this range. The other small peaks at very high sequence length, can either be other signals like nucleolar signals or also annotation errors. Figures for the length distribution of each signal type can be found in the appendix (Figure A1-A3).

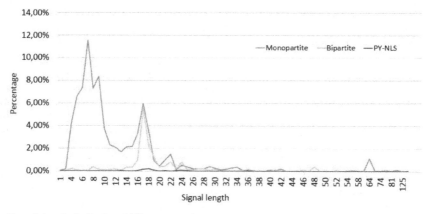

Figure 3: Length distribution of different types of NLSs.
Monopartite signals (2020) are in blue, bipartite signals (413) are in yellow and PY-NLSs (19) are in green.

3.2.2. Organism of origin

Uniprot-IDs are build up with identifier followed by a keyword for the organism the protein belongs to [UniProtID]. These organism keywords were used to investigate the distribution of organism for proteins carrying a NLS.

A first test was made to see the distribution of organisms containing proteins with NLSs within the kingdoms of life. Most proteins with monopartite NLSs were from the virus kingdom (85%), followed by the eukaryotic kingdom (15%). The same distribution was found for proteins with bipartite NLSs (80 % from viruses and 20% from eukaryotic kingdom). The small dataset of PY-NLSs consisted only of proteins from human and yeast. Table 6 shows the distribution of the organism within viruses, bacteria, archaea and eukaryotes. It is remarkable that most proteins with NLSs are from viruses. Viruses are not able to reproduce themselves. They need to enter the nucleus of the host cell and let their genetic material be replicated by the host cell [Campbell2009]. It is possible to assume a connection between the high number of 872 viral proteins carrying a NLS and the biological background of virus reproduction.

Kingdom	Monopartite NLS (698 organisms)	Bipartite NLS (349 organisms)	PY-NLS (2 organisms)
Virus	592 (84.8%)	280 (80%)	0 (0%)
Eukaryota	104 (14.9%)	69 (20%)	2 (100%)
Bacteria	2 (0.3%)	0 (0%)	0 (0%)
Archaea	0 (0%)	0 (0%)	0 (0%)

Table 6: Distribution of organisms for proteins with NLSs in the kingdoms of life.
For example, monopartite NLSs are found in proteins across 698 organisms, of which 592 (84.8%) are viruses, 104 (14.9%) are eukaryotic and 2 (0.3%) are bacteria.

The organism of proteins with NLSs were highly diverse. Monopartite NLSs were found in proteins from 698 different organism, of which 592 were viruses, 104 eukaryotes and 2 bacteria. Proteins with bipartite NLSs in 349 organism were distributed in 280 viruses and 69 eukaryotes. The small dataset for PY-NLSs consisted of proteins from 2 eukaryotic organisms (human and yeast).

Even though there were 698 different organism for monopartite NLSs and 349 organism for bipartite NLSs, almost half of the proteins of both signals types was spread in only 10 different organism. Figure 4 shows a comparison of the organism holding this first half of proteins with monopartite NLSs and bipartite NLSs. Most proteins for monopartite signals were from human and mouse. Many bipartite signals could be found in this two organism, too. However, many bipartite signals were also found in yeast and plants, such as cress and rice. It is possible that bipartite signals are more common in plants or easier to detect in their proteins. To follow these assumptions further tests need to be done.

Another test was done to prove the distribution of proteins with bipartite signals in the 349 different organisms. This test compared the signal length with the organism distribution. Two organism-specific signal length distributions were created. One for all signals from human proteins, and the other for all signals from yeast proteins. The two length distributions for signals exclusively contained in proteins of human and yeast can be found in the appendix (Figure A7 and A8, respectively). These length distributions showed the same characteristic peaks as the length distribution of all signals show in Figure 3. The two organism-specific length distributions showed that the peak for signals from human proteins correspond with the peak in the length distribution of monopartite signals. The peak in the signals of yeast proteins followed the distribution of bipartite and PY-NLSs. Depending on the definition used for classifying yeast and to which group fungi belong, this can be seen as a strengthening of the hypothesis that bipartite NLSs are more common in plant organisms.

These observations indicated that we can trust the organism distribution presented in Figure 4.

Generally, we can see that the proteins carrying a NLS are mostly distributed in model organisms. This is an expected finding. An explanation for the high amount of known signals in human proteins, can be the correlation of NLSs and DNA regulation and diseases.

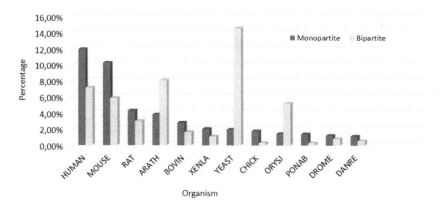

Figure 4: Comparison of organism for proteins with monopartite and bipartite NLSs, shows the distribution of the top 45% of proteins with monopartite (blue bars) and bipartite (yellow bars) across 12 organisms. The single distributions of the top 50% of proteins for each signal type across the different organisms is provided in the appendix (Figure A4-A5).

The result of comparison the organism keyword of the proteins of each signal type separately can be found in the appendix (Figure A4-A6).

3.2.3. Sequence similarity

We investigated protein sequences similarity to answer the question if proteins containing NLSs have a similar sequence. Figure 5 shows the distribution of HSSP values calculated from blast alignments for each protein of a signal type against all proteins from all signals types. More than half of proteins are highly similar in their sequence and have an HSSP value higher than 60. Further, we wanted to know if proteins with similar sequences share similar NLSs. A redundancy reduction and searching of signals in the reduced set was performed. We reduced the proteins sequences regarding to 100%, 80%, 60% and 40% sequence similarity using Cd-hit [Li2001] with c=1.0, 0.8, 0.6 and 0.4, respectively.

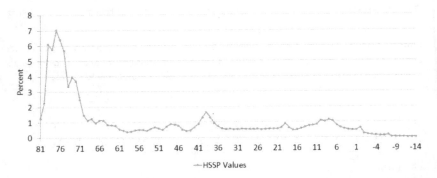

Figure 5: Distribution of HSSP values for the proteins of all NLS types. The top 50% of proteins has an HSSP value higher than 60.

Figure 6 shows the numbers of proteins (blue bars) and unique NLSs (yellow bars) in the sets of 100%, 80%, 60%, 40% und 20% sequence redundancy reduced proteins. The set of proteins with sequences redundancy reduced to 20% was calculated by Uniqueprot [Mika2003] with parameter t = 0. Figure 6 also shows the number of signals found in these protein sets.

At 100% sequence identity we had 3181 proteins from all signal types left with Cd-hit. The signals were matched in this set of protein sequences: 1761 unique signals matched in the 3181 proteins. Sequence identity of 80% dropped the number of proteins to 1424 and the matching signals to 1421. This was the decrease of proteins fitting the top half of very similar proteins that can be also seen in the HSSP curve with a high HVAL (Figure 5). From there on the numbers of proteins and signals dropped slightly. At a sequence identity of 60% 1071 proteins and 1162 signal were left. At 40% the numbers fell to 852 proteins and 1016 signals. The calculation for 20% sequence identity was run by Uniqueprot, because of different algorithm the numbers for 20% were higher than the numbers for 40% calculated by Cd-hit. At 20% sequence identity Uniqueprot left 889 proteins in the set and the number of NLSs found in that is 1012 signals.

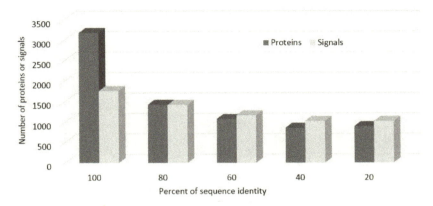

Figure 6: Redundancy reduced sets of proteins (blue bars) and signals (yellow bars) found in those sets by using Cd-hit [Li2001]. The set of 100% sequence identity (c=1.0) contained 3181 proteins. We matched 1761 unique signals in that set. Further reduction to 80%, 60% and 40% (c=0.8, c=0.6 and c=0.4) resulted in 1424, 1071 and 852 proteins, respectively. For 80% sequence identity 1421 signals, for 60% sequence identity 1162 signals and for 40% sequence identity 1016 signals were found to match in the protein sequences. A set for 20%sequence identity was created with Uniqueprot (t=0) [Mika2003]. It contained 889 proteins and 1012 signals matched in that set.

3.2.4. Subcellular localization

Proteins that are imported into the nucleus and have their functional destination within the nucleus and its sub-compartments are expected to have a nuclear location annotation. Therefore, the subcellular location annotation of the proteins containing the signals was investigated.

Localization annotations were extracted from the Swiss-Prot database. All annotation types were considered. Almost for all proteins we found subcellular location annotations in Swiss-Prot. Only 6 proteins of 2652 proteins with monopartite NLSs, 12 proteins of 734 proteins with bipartite NLSs and 1 protein of 17 proteins with PY-NLSs had no annotation. For these proteins a localization prediction was made by LocTree3 [Goldberg2014] using PredictProtein [Yachdav2014]. Predicted subcellular locations were marked with PP. Swiss-Prot often provides multiple location annotations for a protein. We did not consider the number of locations in one annotation. For every protein the subcellular location annotation from Swiss-Prot counted as one annotation.

We found 178 different annotations of locations for proteins with monopartite signals, 45 different location annotations for proteins with bipartite NLSs and 9 location annotations for proteins carrying a PY-NLSs.

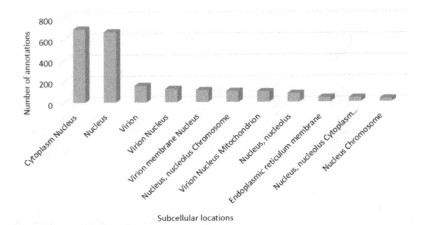

Figure 7: Subcellular locations of 2652 proteins with monopartite NLSs. Annotation for the top 82% of the proteins.

The highest number of proteins with monopartite NLSs was annotated to be located in both cytoplasm and nucleus. Figure 7 shows that the top 82% of proteins with monopartite NLSs were at least partly annotated to be located in the nucleus or its sub-compartments. Only the locations "Virion" and "Endoplasmic reticulum membrane" were annotations that do not imply nuclear activity of the proteins. Fitting to the distribution of proteins with monopartite signals in the kingdoms of life, many proteins were annotated to be located within viral compartments.

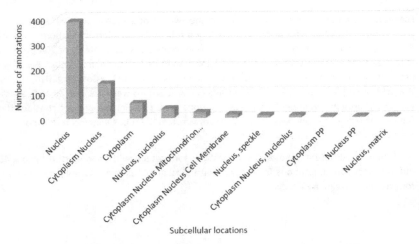

Figure 81: Location annotations for 734 proteins with bipartite NLSs. Annotation for the top 94% of the proteins.

As it was shown in Table 6 the bipartite signals were also distributed in many viral organism (Figure 8). Interestingly, the location annotations did not show viral compartments, other as in the location annotations for proteins with monopartite signals. For proteins with bipartite signals the highest number was clearly annotated to be nuclear, followed by a multiple annotation of cytoplasm and nucleus. Many of the bipartite signals were annotated to be exclusively located in the Cytoplasm or were predicted in it (Cytoplasm PP).

For those proteins annotated in locations exclusively outside the nucleus it can be presumed that they either had also multiple locations and the nuclear localizations was not yet annotated or that they were wrongly annotated in Uniprot.

The proteins of the small dataset of PY-NLSs was mostly annotated to be located in the nucleus, followed by cytoplasm and one location in the cell membrane, see Figure 9.

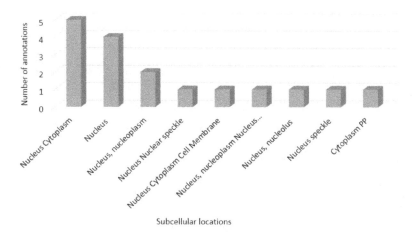

Figure 92: Location annotations for 17 proteins with PY-NLSs.

3.2.5. Clustering of signals

The clustering of monopartite NLSs sequences is presented in Figure 10. The sequences were visualized with a color code for their general amino acid charge. The charge was calculated by averaging all single charges of amino acids in a sequence. The single charges were taken from the AAindex database [Kawashima1999]. According to their similarity the signal sequences were separated into 40 distinct sub-groups. We can see that all sub-clusters fell into one big main cluster. A few sequences colored blue (see bracket in Figure 10) formed a sub-group excluded from the main clusters. We were interested in the definition of a consensus sequence for the signals of this small separate cluster. The signal sequences from this sub-cluster were aligned with Clustal Omega [Sievers2011] and their multiple sequence alignment was provided as input to Weblogo [Crooks2004] to create their consensus sequences.

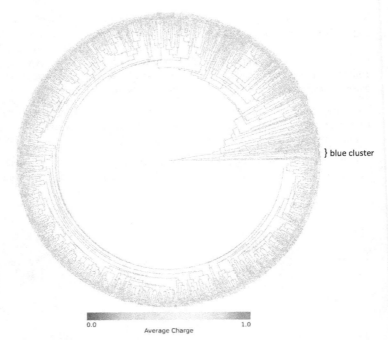

} blue cluster

0.0   1.0
              Average Charge

Figure 10: Clustered monopartite signals. The signals were clustered into sub-groups and colored by the average charge of their amino acids (see legend). Positive charged signals were colored orange-red, neutral signals were colored yellow and the more negatively charged amino acids a signals contained the deeper blue it was colored. The signals were sorted into sub-clusters regarding to their similarity. All sub-clusters, except the blue colored sub-cluster (see bracket), fell into one big main cluster.

Figure 11 shows the logo for the blue sub-cluster of monopartite signals (bracket in Figure 10).

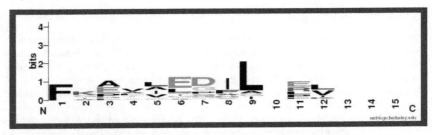

Figure 11: Sequence logo of blue sub-cluster (see bracket Figure 10) Weblogo [Crooks2004].

The amino acids of the small sub-cluster of monopartite NLSs (bracket in Figure 10) tended to be hydrophobic and negatively charged. This is contradictory compared to the classic definition of monopartite signals as a short stretch of basic amino acids. The other clusters were also aligned and visualized. Figure 12 shows sequence logos for 12 randomly chosen groups out of the 40 sub-groups for monopartite NLSs.

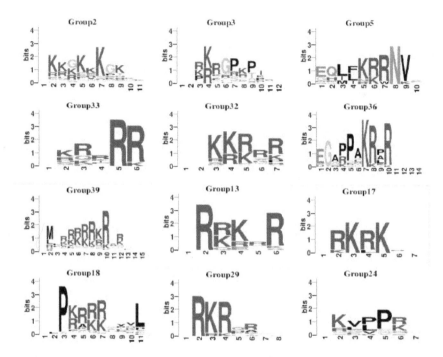

Figure 12: Sequence logos for 12 randomly chosen groups out of 40 sub-groups of monopartite signals visualized by Weblogo [Crooks2004].

While most groups followed the classic definitions of consisting of short stretched of basic amino acids, especially in group 32 and group 17, there are some exemptions. For example, the sequence logo of group 5 looks like the characteristic pattern for a monopartite signal is enclosed by the rest of the signals amino acids. The consensus sequence of group 5 further showed a conserved ending with asparagine followed by valine. The sequence logo for group 18 also looks interesting. In this group the stretch of basic amino acids came directly after a strongly conserved proline and finishes with a leucine. Between the basic pattern and the leucine were some highly variable amino acids. Further investigation of the signals from this sub-group could provide information on the effect of the sequence besides the basic patch of monopartite signals.

The bipartite signals were clustered and according to sub-clusters of similar sequences sorted into sub-groups. In the visualization of the clustering of bipartite signals (Figure 13) the color of the sequences corresponds to the 38 found sub-groups. Here again the signals within distinct sub-groups were aligned and logos created with Weblogo [Crooks2004].

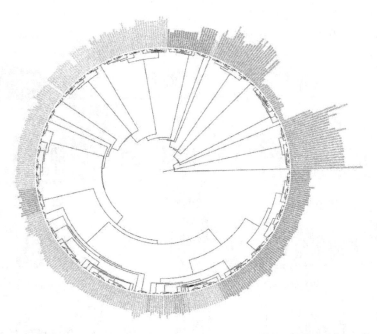

Figure 13: Clustered bipartite signals. The signals are clustered into 38 sub-groups and colored regarding these groups.

Figure 14 shows sequence logos for 12 randomly chosen groups out of the 38 sub-groups for bipartite NLSs.

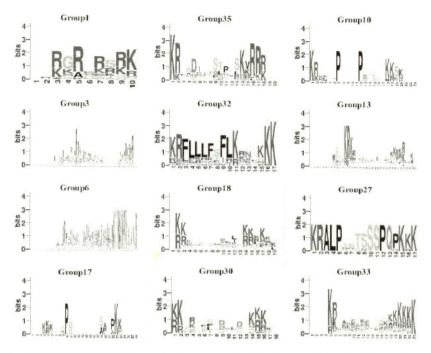

Figure 14: Sequence logos for 12 randomly chosen groups out of 38 sub-groups of bipartite signals visualized by Weblogo [Crooks2004].

The consensus sequence of high diverse signals like the bipartite NLSs were more difficult to visualize as sequence logo. Still, a general observation shows that the logos fit to the consensus rule of bipartite signals. Start and end of the signals were short stretches of basic amino acids and in the middle was a linker part. The sequence logo for group 1 looks more like a group of monopartite signals. The sequences were overall basic, had no clear linker and were too short to be bipartite signals. This could lead from annotation errors in the dataset. The linker sequences of group 35 and group 27 look interesting. They were dominated by polar or negative amino acids. In the sequences of group 27 hydrophobic amino acids came just before these polar/negative ones. A possible biological explanations is that bipartite signals are signal patches. It is possible that the hydrophobic part of the sequence is not part of the signal. When the protein is folded, the basic stretch and the polar residues in between can be on the proteins surface ready for interaction with importin. Group 10, 7 and 27 had a strongly conserved proline at the beginning and end of the linker sequence. Additional to defining consensus sequences or giving a broader view of the signals variability, further investigations based on observations like this can shed light on e.g. possible functions of positions within the linker sequence.

These steps were done for the PY-NLS dataset, also it was very small (17 signals). Figure 15 shows the clustering result. In this chart 5 sub-groups can be detected. This sub-groups were aligned and the logos created.

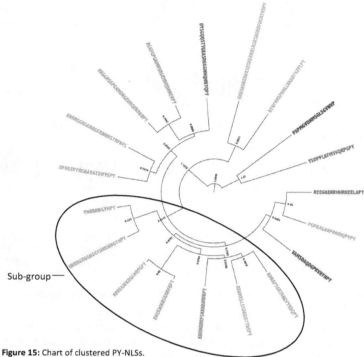

Sub-group —

Figure 15: Chart of clustered PY-NLSs.

Most of the logos created by the sub-clusters of this signal group, did not show significant results, because of the small samples size and the inconstant nature of PY-signals. Figure 16 shows the sequence logo for the fourth sub-group containing 7 signals (see mark in Figure 15).

Figure 16: Sequence logo for a sub-group of PY-NLSs containing 7 signals (see mark in Figure 15).

In this figure the general basic character of these sequences can be seen. The characteristic proline and tyrosine residue at the end of the signals are also visible. In addition, it can be inferred, that the signal start with a basic stretch, that is followed by two linker sequences and a conserved basic stretch of one or more amino acids. This fits to the general description of the PY-NLS sequence.

The logos of all sub-groups for the different signals types can be found in the supplementary material (on the DVD).

3.3. 4301 novel potential NLSs through mutagenesis

Two protein sets were collected from Swiss-Prot to test the occurrence of potential NLSs in 6538 sequence-unique nuclear and 23082 sequence-unique non-nuclear proteins. From the initial set of 2452 experimental signals of different types, only 1419 signals were left not matching in any of the sequences of the non-nuclear data. Out of these 1419 signals only 310 signals matched exclusively in the sequences of the nuclear protein set. These remaining 310 signals were mutated and tested again against the two protein sets. The set of potential NLSs had a size of 4301 signals. Figure 17 visualizes the described process and the numbers of protein and signal sets.

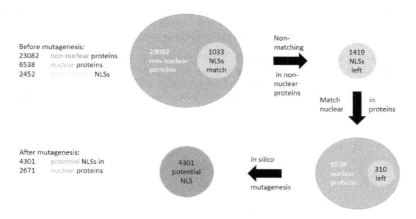

Figure 17: Mutational approach: Numbers of proteins and signals. Before the mutagenesis we had three sets: a set with 23082 non-nuclear proteins, a set with 6538 nuclear proteins and a set with 2452 experimental signals. The signals were matched in the sequences of the non-nuclear proteins. In this set 1033 signals matched and 1419 signals did not match. We used the 1419 signals and matched them in the sequences of the nuclear proteins. The remaining 310 signals matching exclusively in the nuclear protein sequences, were mutated by an *in silico* mutagenesis approach. This led to 4301 potential signals matching in 2641 nuclear proteins.

3.3.1. Characterization of potential NLSs

As mentioned in section 2.3.1., the clusters of monopartite NLSs were used to create sub-groups and sequence logos. These groups were also used to align them against the potential NLSs most similar to them. The alignment of potential signals and monopartite sub-groups was used for the creation of new sequence logos. Using these alignments it is possible to evaluate the following ideas:

If the potential signals are novel not yet discovered signals similar to the signals of the monopartite sub-groups, the sequence logos will show this. A rank score was set by using 10000 random background sequences to evaluate the significance of an alignment score for a potential signal against a monopartite sub-group. A rank of 0 implied that all potential signals with that rank scored better than the random sequences, respectively match significantly in the aligned sub-group. It was possible that sequences of potential signals can have high ranks for several groups. We believe this is mostly due to the background dataset of sequences in which we compare against to obtain a rank. To overcome this in the future we could distinguish between ranks of potential signals for similar groups by instead comparing against the proteome of an organism, e.g., Humans, or by using random sequences with preferences of amino acids found in known NLSs.

Sequence logos helped to visualize high match scores of the alignment of potential signals against sub-groups of monopartite NLSs. It is an interesting observation that *in silico* created potential signals followed the patterns of classic monopartite signals and helped to extend or refine the consensus sequences for each of the monopartite sub-groups.

The following two Figures 18 and 19, are an example for the refinement of consensus sequences for the monopartite sub-groups by aligning them against potential NLSs. The sequence logos for all other monopartite sub-groups, as well as the sequence logos for the monopartite sub-groups aligned against potential NLSs are provided in the appendix (Figures A9-Figures A45).

Figure 18 shows the sequence logo of sub-groups 8 for monopartite NLSs. The groups were consecutively numbered.

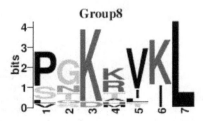

Figure 18: Sequence logo for sub-group 8 of monopartite signals

The sequence logo for groups 8 shows the multiple sequence alignment for 13 sequences of monopartite signals. Starting with a proline and glycine a conservation of basic amino acids in the middle of the signals can be seen.

Figure 19 shows the resulting consensus sequence for the alignment of sub-group 8 of monopartite signals against the potential signals most similar to this group.

Figure 19: Sequence logo for the alignment of sub-group 8 of monopartite signals against potential NLSs most similar to this group.

The consensus sequence for the combined alignment of the signals of sub-group 8 and 53 potential NLSs similar to the sequences of group 8 showed strongly conserved amino acids. The signals started with two proline residues followed by a basic patch of amino acids.

The direct comparison of the Figure 18 and 19 shows that the consensus sequence of the monopartite signals was refined and extended through the alignment against the potential NLSs. Figure 19 further indicates that the consensus sequence was extended with basic amino acids. The consensus sequence reflected the characteristic basic pattern of amino acids in monopartite signals. Additionally, the signal start with two conserved proline residues are a refinement of consensus sequences for monopartite signals that can be proven in further studies. An indicator for the validity of a consensus sequence for monopartite signals starting with a Proline were the experimentally found consensus sequences (Table 2, section 2.1.1.) for class 2 and class 4 of monopartite signals defined by Kosugi *et al.* [Kosugi2008].

Another characteristic of the potential NLSs could be found in their length. The new potential signals tended to be shorter ones. As Figure 20 shows, a few longer signals existed and the rest of the signals were distributed between lengths of 4-10 amino acids. The longest signal was 23 amino acids long. Almost 70% of the signals were 6 amino acids long. This indicates that a sequences with length shorter than 6 amino acids lost the specificity of the signals, because the shorter sequences matched in protein sequences of both the nuclear and non-nuclear set.

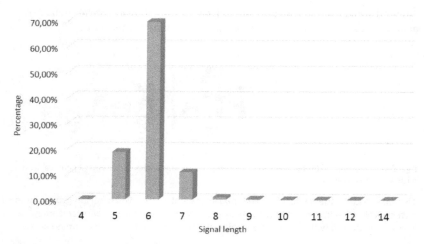

Figure 20: Length distribution of 4301 potential NLSs

3.3.2. Increasing coverage from 9% to 49%

NLSdb2.0 consisted of the 2452 collected experimentally verified NLSs and the 4301 potential NLSs created by *in silico* mutagenesis from this study.

With the signals of NLSdb1.0 the coverage for finding a known nuclear protein was increased from 9% (found NLSs in nuclear proteins by Swiss-Prot) to 43% [Cokol2000]. Repeating this experiment the nuclear protein set annotated by Swiss-Prot containing 6538 protein was used. Swiss-Prot had an annotation for a NLS in 596 unique proteins in the nuclear protein set. In 2000 there were 3142 proteins annotated to be nuclear proteins and 290 of them were marked with a NLS annotation in Swiss-Prot [Cokol2000]. Even though the number of nuclear proteins and the number of NLSs in Swiss-Prot was more than doubled the relation of annotated NLSs in nuclear proteins remained at 9 %. Running PredictNLS with the newly annotated 6538 nuclear proteins showed that the signals of NLSdb1.0 were found in only 19% of the nuclear proteins. A comparison of Uniprot-ACs for those protein sequences in the dataset with either one of the experimental or potential NLSs, with the Uniprot-ACs of the 6538 nuclear proteins showed that 50% of the nuclear proteins can be annotated with the new signals. NLSdb2.0 increased the coverage from 9% to 50%. Additionally, the signals of NLSdb2.0 were matched to the protein sequences of the 6538 nuclear proteins. In 6526 (99%) of the protein sequences a signals from NLSdb2.0 matched concluding that with the signals of NLSdb2.0 all nuclear proteins can be detected.

We also validated the performance of NLSdb2.0 and NLSdb1.0 on 1659 nuclear proteins extracted from all Swiss-Prot proteins annotated before 2000. For extracting the 1659 nuclear proteins we used the same criteria as for the nuclear set of proteins from 2015 described in section 2.2.1. Swiss-Prot covered 10% of the nuclear proteins from the release before 2000 by having an annotation for a NLS in the motif section of 174 proteins. The signals of NLSdb1.0 covered 21% of the 1659 nuclear proteins. In 347 protein sequences a signal from NLSdb1.0 was matched by PredictNLS. We compared the Uniprot-ACs of all proteins containing the experimental and potential signals from NLSdb2.0 with the Uniprot-ACs of the 1659 nuclear proteins. The coverage of the nuclear proteins known before 2000 by NLSdb2.0 was 45%. Additional, the signals of NLSdb2.0 were matched in the protein sequences of the 1659 nuclear protein annotated before 2000. In 1655 of the nuclear protein sequences a signal from NLSdb2.0 was matched, leading to a coverage of 99%.

Table 7 shows the observations of coverage in numbers and percentage.

2015	6538 nuclear proteins	2000	1659 nuclear proteins
Swiss-Prot	598 (9%)		174 (10%)
NLSdb1.0	1261 (19%)		347 (21%)
NLSdb2.0	3259 (50%)		755 (45%)

Table 7: Coverage of known nuclear proteins annotated by NLS motifs. The set of experimentally verified nuclear proteins contained 6538 sequences. Swiss-Prot annotated a NLS for 598 proteins of the nuclear proteins. The coverage for Swiss-Prot on nuclear proteins was 9%. The signals of NLSdb1.0 matched in 1261 sequences of the nuclear proteins, this corresponded to a coverage of 19%. The signals of NLSdb2.0 matched in 3259 proteins of the nuclear proteins, corresponding to 49% coverage of nuclear proteins. NLSdb2.0 raised the coverage of nuclear proteins annotated by NLSs from 9% to 49%. A Swiss-Prot release published before 2000 was used to compare the coverage of the nuclear proteins known in 2015 to the coverage of the nuclear proteins known in 2003, when NLSdb1.0 was published. From this release we extracted 1659 experimentally verified nuclear proteins. In 174 proteins of these 1659 nuclear proteins Swiss-Prot had an annotation of a NLS in the motif section. This covered 10% of the nuclear proteins. The signals of NLSdb1.0 were found in 347 nuclear proteins, covering 21%. The signals of NLSdb2.0 found 755 nuclear proteins, covering 45% of the nuclear proteins. NLSdb2.0 outperforms the coverage of nuclear proteins found by Swiss-Prot and NLSsb1.0.

3.4. Benchmark – NLSdb1.0 vs. NLSdb2.0

For benchmarking NLSdb1.0 with NLSdb2.0 we used 6545 unique proteins found to have experimental and potential NLSs from our dataset. Each protein of each type of NLSs was then inputted into PredictNLS.

3.4.1. 38% of proteins with novel potential NLSs in NLSdb1.0

The numbers of proteins having NLSs of a specific type were the following: Proteins with monopartite NLSs: 2652; proteins with bipartite NLSs: 734; proteins with PY-NLSs: 17 and proteins with potential: 3142. PredictNLS found signals in 865 proteins of the monopartite set (43%), in 389 proteins of the bipartite set (53%), in 9 of the PY-signal containing proteins (47%) and in 945 of the proteins where a potential NLS was matched (30%). This is shown in Table 8.

Signal type	Number of proteins in NLSdb2.0	Number of proteins in NLSdb1.0	Proteins from NLSdb2.0 found in NLSdb1.0
Monopartite NLS	2652	1131	43%
Bipartite NLS	734	389	53%
PY-NLS	19	9	47%
Potential NLS	3142	945	30%
All NLSs	6574	2474	38%

Table 8: With PredictNLS 38% of proteins with signals of NLSdb2.0 were predicted to contain a NLS.

Overall 38% of proteins containing the signals of NLSdb2.0 were predicted to have a NLS with PredictNLS. PredictNLS performed well on the protein sets containing bipartite and PY-NLSs. The result that PredictNLS found only 38% of proteins with the new experimental and potential signals shows how many more signals and proteins could be found more than 10 years after NLSdb1.0 was introduced.

3.4.2. 100% overlap between NLSdb1.0 and NLSdb 2.0

From Swiss-Prot 22436 proteins from eukaryotic organism were collected without having an annotation for subcellular location. The proteins were redundancy reduced with Uniqueprot [Mika2003] to a set having only 20% sequence identity. The reduced set size was 1746 proteins. They were used both to match the experimental and potential NLSs from this study and to run PredictNLS with them. In 1410 proteins a NLS from NLSdb2.0 was found. PredictNLS found a NLS from NLSdb1.0 in 58 proteins. All proteins found by PredictNLS were also found with the signals of NLSdb2.0. Accordingly, the overlap of these two versions is 100%. This result is visualized in Table 9.

1746 unique proteins with no location annotation in Swiss-Prot	Number of found proteins	Percentage of found proteins
Proteins with signals from NLSdb1.0	58	3.3%
Proteins with signals from NLSdb2.0	1411	81%
Proteins found with signals in NLSdb1.0 and NLSdb2.0	58	100%

Table 9: Found proteins with NLSs in a set of 1746 proteins with no location annotation in Swiss-Prot. NLSdb1.0 found signals in 58 proteins with no location annotation, predicting only 3.3% of proteins to be nuclear. NLSdb2.0 found 1411 proteins of the unannotated protein set to contain a NLS. NLSdb2.0 predicted 81% of the unannotated proteins to be nuclear. The 58 proteins found with the signals of NLSdb1.0 were included in the 1411 proteins found with the signals of NLSdb2.0. The overlap of the NLSdb1.0 and NLSdb2.0 is 100%.

To validate the prediction of nuclear localization of proteins matching a potential NLS, we randomly chose 5 proteins from this set. We searched the literature for an experimental evidence for the protein to be nuclear. Table 10 summarizes the findings of this analysis.

Protein ID	Gene name	Citation for nuclear evidence
Q0IIX4	Smap	The results suggest that SMAP/KAP3 serves as a linker between HCAP and KIF3A/B in the nucleus, and that SMAP/KAP3 plays a role in the interaction of chromosomes with an ATPase motor protein [Shimizu1998].
P62120	RPL41	By immunofluorescence staining, RPL41 induced ATF4 relocation

		from nuclei to cytoplasm, where ATF4 co-stained with a proteasome marker [Wang2011];
Q67YC0	pS2	pS2 was highly expressed in prostate carcinoma (91.4%) with both cytoplasmic and nuclear patterns of staining [Abdou2008].
Q9LIJ4	VP22-2	VP22 found in infected cells is distributed in at least three distinct subcellular localizations, which we define as cytoplasmic, diffuse, and nuclear, as measured by indirect immunofluorescence [Pomeranz1999].
O22431	PRL10	Besides being a constituent of ribosomes and participating in protein translation, additional extra ribosomal functions in the nucleus have been described for RPL10 in different organisms. [Ferreyra2013].

Table 10: Citations of nuclear location annotations for proteins found to have a NLS by NLSdb2.0

While searching for experimental nuclear annotations for the proteins found to have a NLS, it often appeared that ribosomal subunits have additional functions in the nucleus. The two proteins RPL41 and RPL10 strengthen this statement. It is worth to keep attention on those ribosomal proteins in relation to proteins with acting in the nucleus and nuclear transport signals.

4. Conclusion

The collected data of NLSs, NESs and artificial signals as well as the information about them will be a multiple usable source of signals of protein transported in and out of the nucleus.

The detection of new potential signals and the usability to predict nuclear localizations of proteins, proven by literature is a time and cost saving approach that fulfills the philosophy of bioinformatics as a more efficient way of doing science.

Results of different test for analyzing the signals and their proteins show that on the one hand there are characteristic points that might be generalized but on the other hand the signals differ strongly even within the special groups of monopartite, bipartite and PY-NLSs. For each of this groups an interval of the signals length can be assigned and consensus rules show a general trend of the amino acid arrangement and preferences. The protein distribution in terms of organism is highly diverse and show a high number of proteins from viruses. The similarity of proteins shows that they tend to be homolog, which is conform to the fact, that there is a special group of proteins being functional in the nucleus. The location annotations of the NLSs containing proteins are surprising. Even though the highest part of proteins is annotated to be located in the nucleus and its sub-compartments, there are many proteins left annotated to be localized in other organelles and their membranes. Furthermore, the clustering of signals leads to a definition of sub-groups for the signals types and consensus sequences for these sub-groups.

The clustering of the potential signals with the sub-groups of monopartite signals shows that they are, due to the mutagenesis algorithm, as diverse as the experimental signals. Using the potential signals for an extension of monopartite sub-groups we could refine their consensus sequences and investigate the potential signal patterns.

Coming to the main goal of this work: The update of NLSdb1.0. As seen in the benchmarking, the numbers show that the goal of an improvement was reached. The second version of NLSdb contains a higher number of signals that increase the coverage of nuclear protein from 9% to 49%. It is also able to detect all nuclear proteins that can be found by the signals of NLSdb1.0 and include recent signal types detected after the first publications in 2003.

So all in all the work done in the area of a basic yet important molecular mechanism leads to a highly qualified update of NLSdb. It reflects the current state of science in the area of nuclear transport signals, as well as knowledge and results that can be used in further studies.

5. Outlook

Started as a collaboration project of Rostlab from TU Munich in Munich Germany and Mikael Bodén´s Lab from the University of Queensland in Brisbane Australia the work done in this study will be continued in the future. The restricted time of a bachelor thesis is by far not enough to finish all interesting steps. There are several things already planned to work on as well as presumptions that might be investigated or ideas for further projects.

Definitely planned is the analyses of nuclear export signals. All steps outlined in the material and methods section can be repeated for analyses of NESs. Additionally to that, the existing datasets can be further increased by the mentioned remaining sources and left out searching parameters. For both NLSs and NESs can be done a statistics of Gene Ontology terms, similar to the statistics of subcellular location. This would lead to a better characterization of the functions of proteins with the signals. To update NLSdb1.0 a new user interface will be set up and the database of signals found in this study will be included once the collections and analyses are finished.

Besides finishing this project, some results lead to presumptions that might be tested and proven. The high distribution of proteins with a NLS coming from viruses, can be just of the explained biological reason. Anyway, statistical and significance proving tests can be done on the data to justify the high number of NLSs in viruses only in the necessity of entering the hosts nucleus.

Another point that arose by observations is the fact that bipartite signals in our data were more often found in plant proteins. If this contributes to annotation or research parameters of the used data or really is a biological fact, can be investigated in the future.

Likewise, worth a second check is the length distribution of the signals. It can be cleared if there are either annotation errors or if the length in each signal truly varies and overlaps like it is shown.

As said before in this thesis, all areas of biology that are related to proteins functioning in the nuclear are potential topics to use the results of this work for further studies. The destination of proteins transported into the nucleus, can be the DNA. So the mechanism that deal with regulation or processing of DNA are all related to proteins having nuclear transport signals. Allergic reactions and diseases are just an example of the subjects that can be studied together with nuclear transport factors, their proteins and properties.

6. Appendix

Sources	NLSdb1.0 (975 proteins)	Lange (68 proteins)	SeqNLS (93 proteins	Swiss-Prot (3874 proteins)	PY-NLS (17 proteins)	All sources (5027 proteins)
Overlap						
NLSdb1.0		5	4	209	1	
Lange			4	2	0	
SeqNLS				11	1	
Swiss-Prot					3	
PY-NLS						
Additional to NLSdb1.0						4031

Table A 1: Comparison of protein ACs from different sources with NLS containing proteins. Combining the proteins of all sources we got 5027 proteins. Between the sources some of the signals overlapped. From the proteins of NLSdb1.0 209 proteins were found in the data collected from Swiss-Prot. An overlap of 5 proteins with Lange *et al.*, 4 proteins with SeqNLS and 1 protein of the PY-NLS was discovered. The proteins from Lange *et al.* and SeqNLS overlapped in 4 proteins and had both an overlap with the signals extracted from Swiss-Prot, of 2 and 11 proteins, respectively. The proteins with PY-NLSs also overlapped with proteins from SeqNLS in 1 protein and in 3 proteins from Swiss-Prot. The field "Additional to NLSdb1.0" lists 4032 unique signals collected in this study. This number is without the proteins of NLSdb1.0 and without the overlapping signals between all sources (in total 21 unique proteins overlapped).

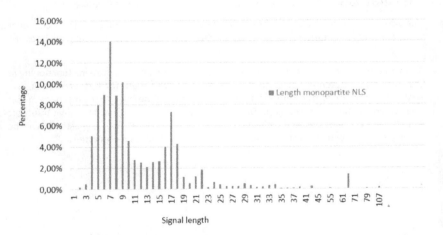

Figure A 1: Length distribution of 2020 monopartite signals.

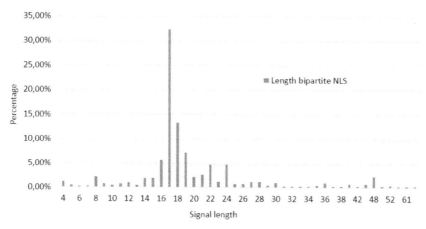

Figure A 2: Length distribution of 413 bipartite signals.

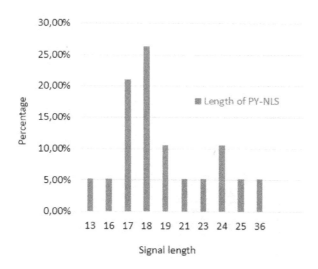

Figure A 3: Length distribution of 19 PY-NLSs.

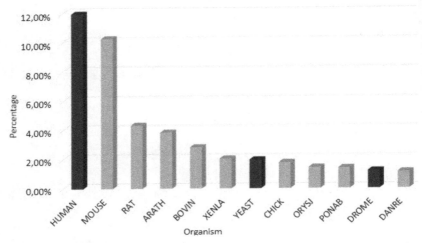

Figure A 4: Organism distribution for top 44% of 2652 proteins with monopartite signals. Human, yeast and drome are colored in dark blue, because proteins from these organism had also signals in NLSdb1.0.

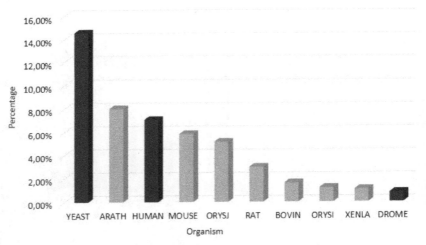

Figure A 5: Organism distribution for top 48% of 734 proteins with bipartite signals. Yeast, human and drome are colored in dark blue, because proteins from these organism had also signals in NLSdb1.0.

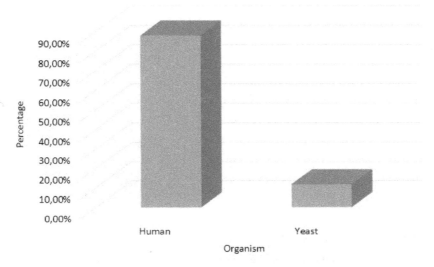

Figure A 6: Organism distribution for 17 proteins with PY-NLSs.

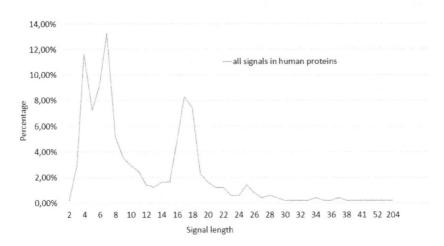

Figure A 7: Length distribution of all signals in 458 human proteins.

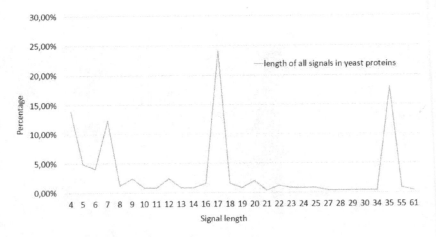

Figure A 8: Length distribution of all signals in 162 yeast proteins.

The following figures all show the sequence logos by alignment of sub-groups of monopartite NLSs, as well as the alignment of the sub-groups against potential NLSs with the highest similarity to that sub-group. The two figures on top are the alignments for the sequences in the sub-group of monopartite NLSs. The logos were created by Weblogo [Crooks2004]. In the left logos the option "small sample size correction" was turned on. This reduced overestimation of single positions due to a small amount of sequences. The logos on the right show the uncorrected versions. The bottom logos show the alignment against the potential NLSs. A possible refinement of the consensus sequence for the sub-group can be investigated. Note, that for sub-groups 5, 9 and 26 no potential NLSs with high similarity were found. For some groups, the small sample correction lead to no sequence logo.

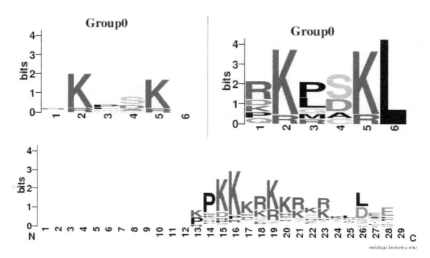

Figure A 9: Sequence logos for monopartite signals of sub-group 0 and the alignment of the sequences of sub-group 0 against potential NLSs most similar to the sequences in this sub-group.

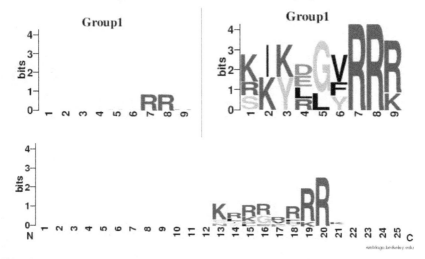

Figure A 10: Sequence logos for monopartite signals of sub-group 1 and the alignment of the sequences of sub-group 1 against potential NLSs most similar to the sequences in this sub-group.

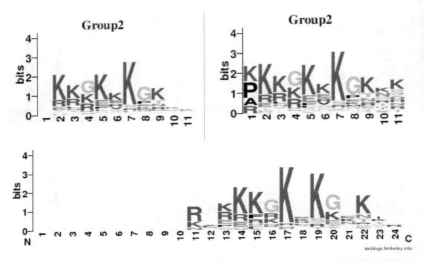

Figure A 11: Sequence logos for monopartite signals of sub-group 2 and the alignment of the sequences of sub-group 2 against potential NLSs most similar to the sequences in this sub-group.

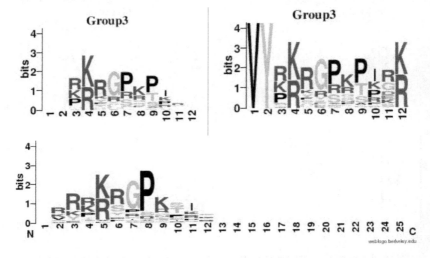

Figure A 12: Sequence logos for monopartite signals of sub-group 3 and the alignment of the sequences of sub-group 3 against potential NLSs most similar to the sequences in this sub-group.

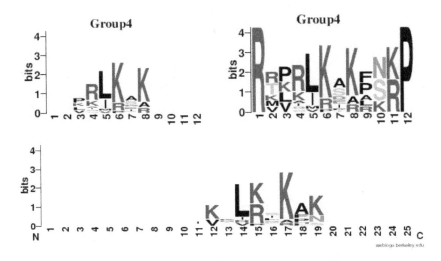

Figure A 13: Sequence logos for monopartite signals of sub-group 4 and the alignment of the sequences of sub-group 4 against potential NLSs most similar to the sequences in this sub-group.

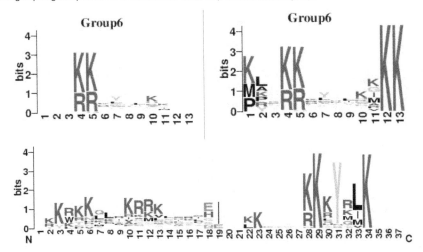

Figure A 14: Sequence logos for monopartite signals of sub-group 6 and the alignment of the sequences of sub-group 6 against potential NLSs most similar to the sequences in this sub-group.

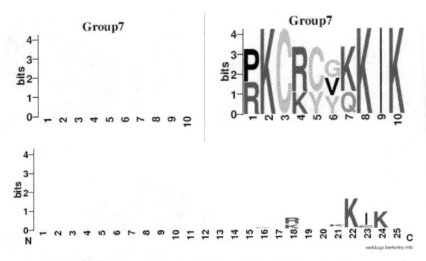

Figure A 15: Sequence logos for monopartite signals of sub-group 7 and the alignment of the sequences of sub-group 7 against potential NLSS most similar to the sequences in this sub-group.

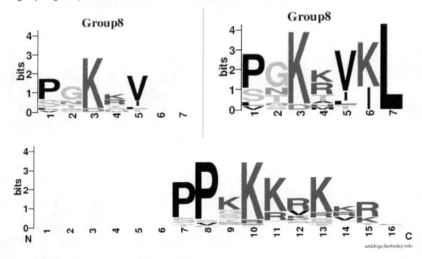

Figure A 16: Sequence logos for monopartite signals of sub-group 8 and the alignment of the sequences of sub-group 8 against potential NLSS most similar to the sequences in this sub-group.

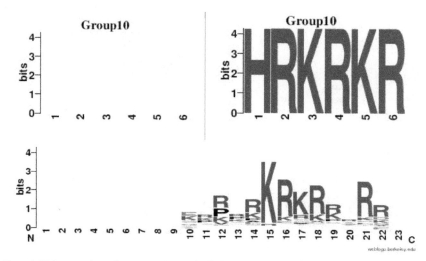

Figure A 17: Sequence logos for monopartite signals of sub-group 10 and the alignment of the sequences of sub-group 10 against potential NLSS most similar to the sequences in this sub-group.

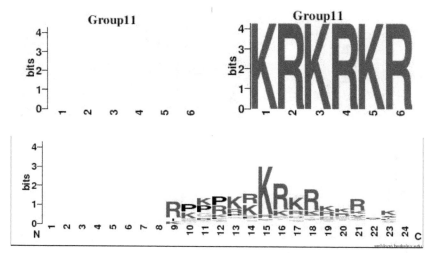

Figure A 18: Sequence logos for monopartite signals of sub-group 11 and the alignment of the sequences of sub-group 11 against potential NLSS most similar to the sequences in this sub-group.

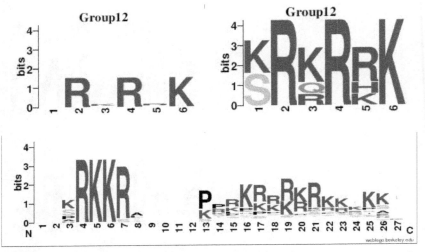

Figure A 19: Sequence logos for monopartite signals of sub-group 12 and the alignment of the sequences of sub-group 12 against potential NLSS most similar to the sequences in this sub-group.

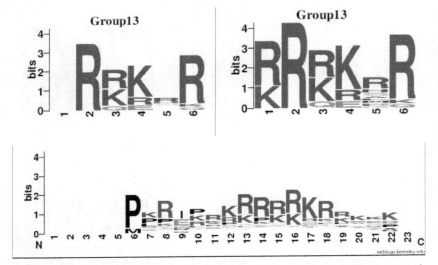

Figure A 20: Sequence logos for monopartite signals of sub-group 13 and the alignment of the sequences of sub-group 13 against potential NLSS most similar to the sequences in this sub-group.

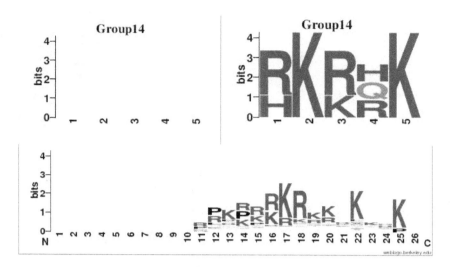

Figure A 21: Sequence logos for monopartite signals of sub-group 14 and the alignment of the sequences of sub-group 14 against potential NLSS most similar to the sequences in this sub-group.

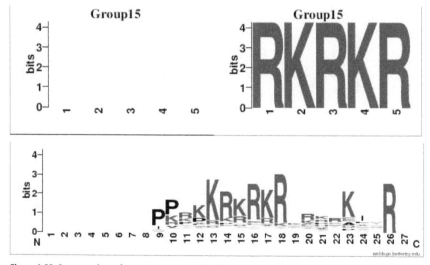

Figure A 22: Sequence logos for monopartite signals of sub-group 15 and the alignment of the sequences of sub-group 15 against potential NLSS most similar to the sequences in this sub-group.

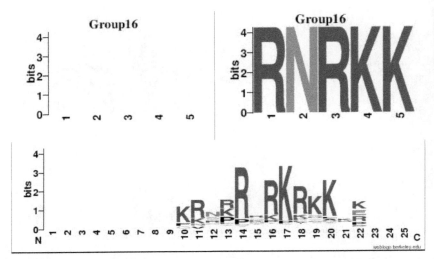

Figure A 23: Sequence logos for monopartite signals of sub-group 16 and the alignment of the sequences of sub-group 16 against potential NLSS most similar to the sequences in this sub-group.

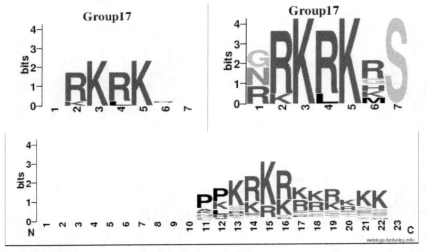

Figure A 24: Sequence logos for monopartite signals of sub-group 17 and the alignment of the sequences of sub-group 17 against potential NLSS most similar to the sequences in this sub-group.

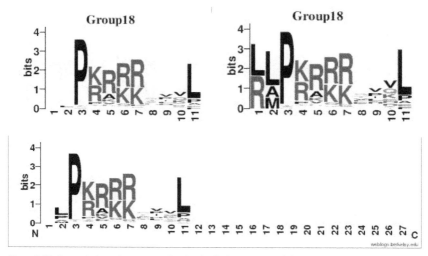

Figure A 25: Sequence logos for monopartite signals of sub-group 18 and the alignment of the sequences of sub-group 18 against potential NLSS most similar to the sequences in this sub-group.

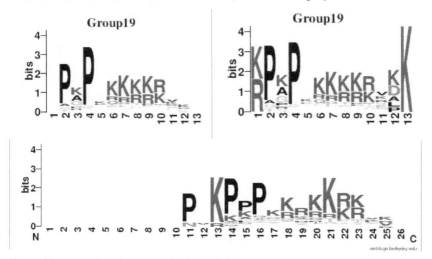

Figure A 26: Sequence logos for monopartite signals of sub-group 19 and the alignment of the sequences of sub-group 19 against potential NLSS most similar to the sequences in this sub-group.

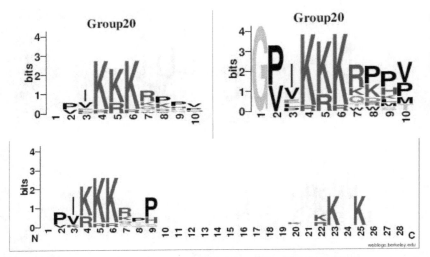

Figure A 27: Sequence logos for monopartite signals of sub-group 20 and the alignment of the sequences of sub-group 20 against potential NLSS most similar to the sequences in this sub-group.

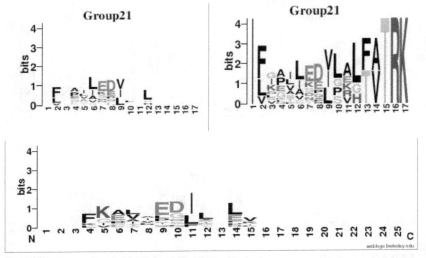

Figure A 28: Sequence logos for monopartite signals of sub-group 21 and the alignment of the sequences of sub-group 21 against potential NLSS most similar to the sequences in this sub-group.

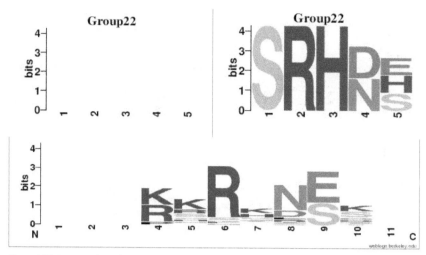

Figure A 29: Sequence logos for monopartite signals of sub-group 22 and the alignment of the sequences of sub-group 22 against potential NLSS most similar to the sequences in this sub-group.

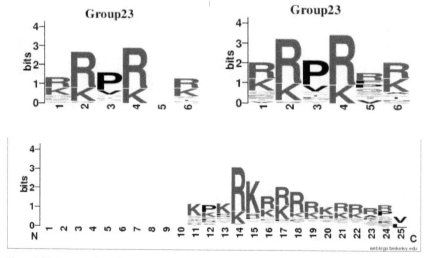

Figure A 30: Sequence logos for monopartite signals of sub-group 23 and the alignment of the sequences of sub-group 23 against potential NLSS most similar to the sequences in this sub-group.

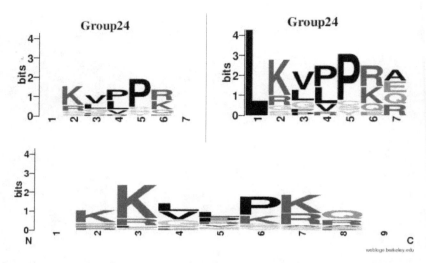

Figure A 31: Sequence logos for monopartite signals of sub-group 24 and the alignment of the sequences of sub-group 24 against potential NLSS most similar to the sequences in this sub-group.

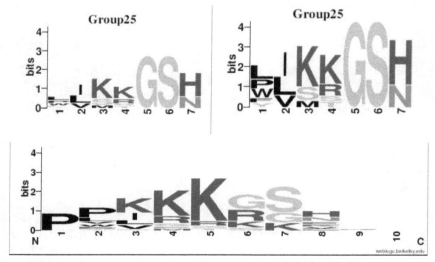

Figure A 32: Sequence logos for monopartite signals of sub-group 25 and the alignment of the sequences of sub-group 25 against potential NLSS most similar to the sequences in this sub-group.

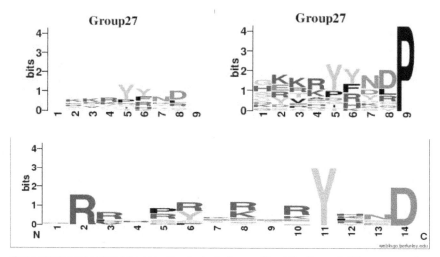

Figure A 33: Sequence logos for monopartite signals of sub-group 27 and the alignment of the sequences of sub-group 27 against potential NLSS most similar to the sequences in this sub-group.

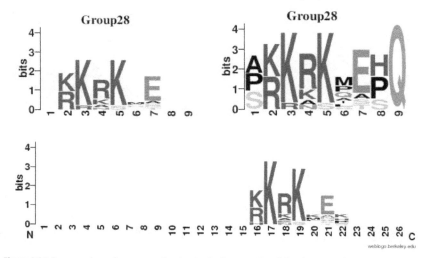

Figure A 34: Sequence logos for monopartite signals of sub-group 28 and the alignment of the sequences of sub-group 28 against potential NLSS most similar to the sequences in this sub-group.

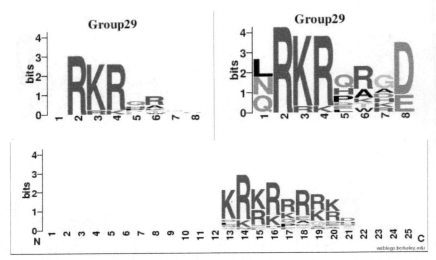

Figure A 35: Sequence logos for monopartite signals of sub-group 29 and the alignment of the sequences of sub-group 29 against potential NLSS most similar to the sequences in this sub-group.

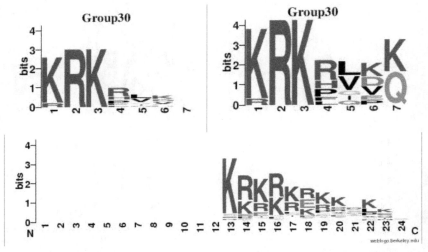

Figure A 36: Sequence logos for monopartite signals of sub-group 30 and the alignment of the sequences of sub-group 30 against potential NLSS most similar to the sequences in this sub-group.

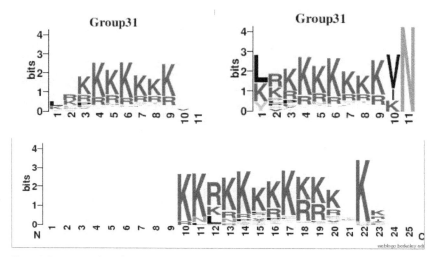

Figure A 37: Sequence logos for monopartite signals of sub-group 31 and the alignment of the sequences of sub-group 31 against potential NLSS most similar to the sequences in this sub-group.

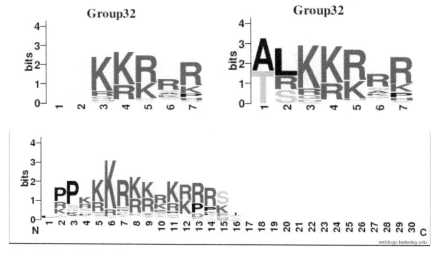

Figure A 38: Sequence logos for monopartite signals of sub-group 32 and the alignment of the sequences of sub-group 32 against potential NLSS most similar to the sequences in this sub-group.

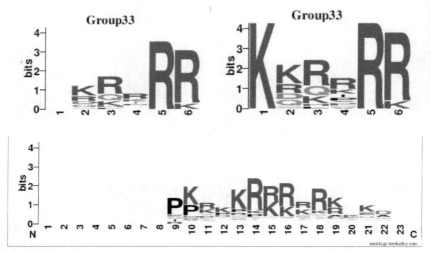

Figure A 39: Sequence logos for monopartite signals of sub-group 33 and the alignment of the sequences of sub-group 33 against potential NLSS most similar to the sequences in this sub-group.

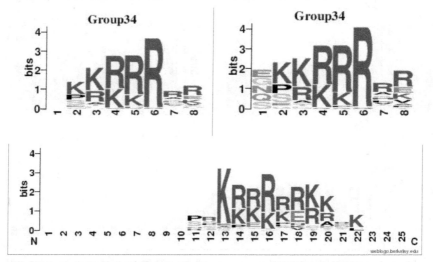

Figure A 40: Sequence logos for monopartite signals of sub-group 34 and the alignment of the sequences of sub-group 34 against potential NLSS most similar to the sequences in this sub-group.

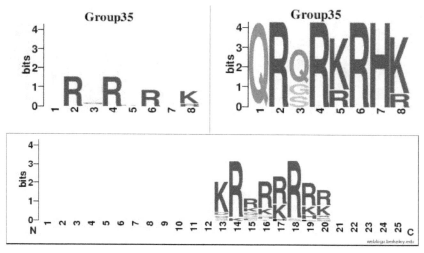

Figure A 41: Sequence logos for monopartite signals of sub-group 35 and the alignment of the sequences of sub-group 35 against potential NLSS most similar to the sequences in this sub-group.

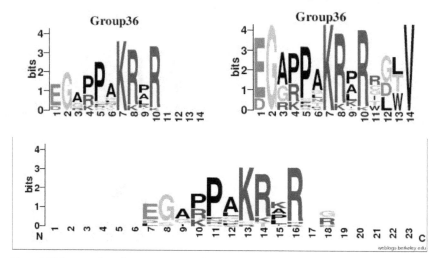

Figure A 42: Sequence logos for monopartite signals of sub-group 36 and the alignment of the sequences of sub-group 36 against potential NLSS most similar to the sequences in this sub-group.

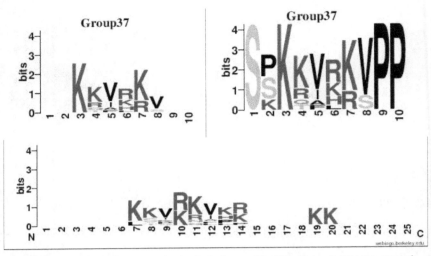

Figure A 43: Sequence logos for monopartite signals of sub-group 37 and the alignment of the sequences of sub-group 37 against potential NLSS most similar to the sequences in this sub-group.

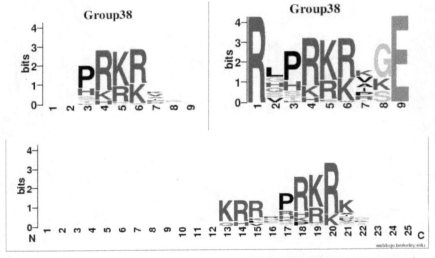

Figure A 44: Sequence logos for monopartite signals of sub-group 38 and the alignment of the sequences of sub-group 38 against potential NLSS most similar to the sequences in this sub-group.

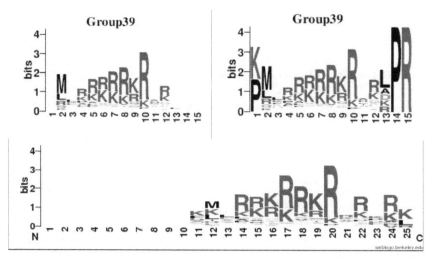

Figure A 45: Sequence logos for monopartite signals of sub-group 39 and the alignment of the sequences of sub-group 39 against potential NLSS most similar to the sequences in this sub-group.

Further material can be found in the supplementary material (on the DVD).

8. References

[Abdou2008]   ASMAA GABER ABDOU, HAYAM ABDEL SAMIE AIAD, SULTAN MOHAMED SULTAN, **pS2 (TFF1) expression in prostate carcinoma: correlation with steroid receptor status**, Apmis (2008) 116:961-971.

[Aggarwal2014]Aggarwal A, Agrawal DK, **Importins and exportins regulating allergic immune responses**, Mediators Inflamm (2014).

[Altschul1990] Altschul SF, Gish W, Miller W, Myers EW, Lipman DJ, **Basic local alignment search tool**, JMol Biol. (1990) 215(3):403-10.

[Aryamontri2015]   Chatr-Aryamontri A, Breitkreutz BJ, Oughtred R, Boucher L, Heinicke S, Chen D, Stark C, Breitkreutz A, Kolas N, O'Donnell L, Reguly T, Nixon J, Ramage L, Winter A, Sellam A, Chang C, Hirschman J, Theesfeld C, Rust J, Livstone MS, Dolinski K, Tyers M, **The BioGRID interaction database: 2015 update**, Nucleic Acids Research (2015) 43:470-8.

[Ba2009]   Alex N Nguyn Ba, Anastassia Pogoutse, Nicholas Provart, Alan M Moses, **NLStradamus: a simple Hidden Markov Model for nuclear localization signal prediction**, BMC Bioinformatics (2009) 10:202.

[Bairoch2004] Bairoch A., Boeckmann B., Ferro S., Gasteiger E. **Swiss-Prot: juggling between evolution and stability**, Brief. Bioinform. (2004) 5:39-55.

[Benson2013] Benson DA, Cavanaugh M, Clark K, Karsch-Mizrachi I, Lipman DJ, Ostell J, Sayers EW, **GenBank.**, Nucleic Acid Research (2013) 41:36-42.

[Bickmore2002]   Wendy A. Bickmore, Heidi G. E. Sutherland, **Addressing protein localization within the nucleus**, The EMBO Journal (2002) 6:1248-1254.

[Cautain2014] Bastien Cautain, Richard Hill, Nuria de Pedro,Wolfgang Link, **Components and regulation of nuclear transport processes**, FEBS Journal (2014) 282:445-462.

[Campbell2009] Neil A.Campbell, Jane B.Reece, **Biologie**, Pearson (2009) 507-526.

[Chibucos2014]Chibucos MC, Mungall CJ, Balakrishnan R, Christie KR, Huntley RP, White O, Blake JA, Lewis SE, Giglio M, **Standardized description of scientific evidence using the Evidence Ontology (ECO)**, Database (Oxford) (2014).

[Cokol2000]   Murat Cokol, Rajesh Nair and Burkhard Rost, **Finding nuclear localization signals**, EMBO Reports (2000) 411-415.

[Colledge1986] W. H. COLLEDGE, W. D. RICHARDSON, M. D. EDGE, ALAN E. SMITH, **Extensive Mutagenesis of the Nuclear Location Signal of Simian Virus 40 Large-T Antigen**, Molecular and Cellular Biology (1986) 4136-4139.

[Cour2003]   Tanja la Cour, Ramneek Gupta, Kristoffer Rapacki, Karen Skriver, Flemming M. Poulsen, Søren Brunak, **NESbase version 1.0: a database of nuclear export signals**, Oxford University Press (2003) 31: 393-396.

[Crooks2004] Gavin E. Crooks, Gary Hon, John-Marc Chandonia, Steven E. Brenner, **WebLogo: A Sequence Logo Generator**, Genome Research (2004) 14:1188–1190.

[Curmi2010]   Paul M. Curmi, Jade K. Forwood, Mikael Bodén, Bostjan Kobe, **Molecular basis for specificity of nuclear import and prediction of nuclear localization**, Biochimica et Biophysica Acta 1813 (2011) 1562–1577.

[Dong2009]   Xiuhua Dong, Anindita Biswas, Katherine E. Süel, Laurie K. Jackson, Rita Martinez, Hongmei Gu, Yuh Min Chook, **Structural basis for leucine-rich nuclear export signal recognition by CRM1**, Nature (2009) 458(7242): 1136–1141.

[Evidence2014] http://www.uniprot.org/help/evidences

[Ferreyra2013] María Lorena Falcone Ferreyra, Romina Casadevall, Marianela Dana Luciani, Alejandro Pezza, Paula Casati, **New Evidence for Differential Roles of L10 Ribosomal Proteins from Arabidopsis**, Plant Physiology (2013) 163:378-391.

[Fischer1995]   Utz Fischer, Jochen Huber, Wilbert C. Boelens, Iain W. Mattaj, Reinhard Lührmann, **The HIV-1 Rev Activation Domain Is a Nuclear Export Signal That Accesses an Export Pathway Used by Specific Cellular RNAs**, Cell (1995) 82:475-483.

[Fornerod1997]Maarten Fornerod, Mutsuhito Ohno, Minoru Yoshida, Iain W. Mattaj, **CRM1 Is an Export Receptor for Leucine-Rich Nuclear Export Signals**, Cell(1997) 90: 1051–1060.

[Fu2011]   Szu-Chin Fu, Kenichiro Imai, Paul Horton, **Prediction of leucine-rich nuclear export signal containing proteins with NESsential**, Nucleic Acids Research (2011) 1–12.

[Fu2012]   Szu-Chin Fu, Hsuan-Cheng Huang, Paul Horton, Hsueh-Fen Juan, **ValidNESs: a database of validated leucine-rich nuclear export signals**, Nucleic Acids Research (2013) 41: 338-343.

[Goldberg2014]   Tatyana Goldberg, Maximilian Hecht, Tobias Hamp, TimothyKarl, Guy Yachdav, Nadeem Ahmed, Uwe Altermann, Philipp Angerer, Sonja Ansorge, Kinga Balasz, Michael Bernhofer, Alexander Betz, Laura Cizmadija, KieuTrinhDo, Julia Gerke, Robert Greil, Vadim Joerdens, Maximilian Hastreiter, Katharina Hembach, Max Herzog,Maria Kalemanov, Michael Kluge, Alice Meier, Hassan Nasir, Ulrich Neumaier,Verena Prade, Jonas Reeb, Aleksandr Sorokoumov, Ilira Troshani, Susann Vorberg, Sonja Waldraff, Jonas Zierer, Henrik Nielsen, Burkhard Rost, **LocTree3 prediction of localization**, Nucleic Acids Research (2014) 42: 350–355.

[Katoh2002]   Katoh, Misawa, Kuma, Miyata, **MAFFT: a novel method for rapid multiple sequence alignment based on fast Fourier transform**, Nucleic Acids Res. (2002) 30:3059-3066.

[Kawashima1999]   Kawashima S, Ogata H, Kanehisa M., **AAindex: Amino Acid Index Database.**, Nucleic Acid Research (1999) 27(1):368-369.

[Kosugi2008]   Shunichi Kosugi, Masako Hasebe, Nobutaka Matsumura, Hideaki Takashima, Etsuko, Miyamoto-Sato, Masaru Tomita, Hiroshi Yanagawa, **Six Classes of Nuclear Localization Signals Specific to Different Binding Grooves of Importin α**, J.Biol.Chem (2009) 284: 478-485.

[Kosugi2.2008] Shunichi Kosugi, Masako Hasebe, Masaru Tomita, Hiroshi Yanagawa, **Nuclear Export Signal Consensus Sequences Defined Using a Localization-Based Yeast Selection System**, Traffic (2008) 9: 2053–2062.

[Kosugi3.2008] Shunichi Kosugi, Masako Hasebe, Masaru Tomita, Hiroshi Yanagawa, **Nuclear Export Signal Consensus Sequences Defined Using a Localization-Based Yeast Selection System**, Traffic (2008) 9: 2053–2062.

[Kosugi2014]   Shunichi Kosugi, Hiroshi Yanagawa, Ryohei Terauchi, Satoshi Tabata, **NESmapper: Accurate Prediction of Leucine-Rich Nuclear Export Signals Using Activity-Based Profiles**, PLOS (2014) 10.

[Krause2005] Antje Krause, Jens Stoye, Martin Vingron, **Large scale hierarchical clustering of protein sequences**, BMC Bioinformatics (2005) 6:15.

[Lange2007] Allison Lange, Ryan E. Mills, Christopher J. Lange, Murray Stewart, Scott E. Devine, Anita H. Corbett, **Classical Nuclear Localization Signals: Definition, Function, and Interaction with Importin α**, J.Biol.Chem (2007) 282: 5101-5105.

[Lange2008] Allison Lange, Ryan E. Mills, Scott E. Devine, Anita H. Corbett, **A PY-NLS Nuclear Targeting Signal Is Required for Nuclear Localization and Function of the Saccharomyces cerevisiae mRNA-binding Protein Hrp1**, J.Biol.Chem (2008) 283: 12926-12934.

[Lee2006] Brittany J. Lee, Ahmet E. Cansizogl, Katherine E. Süel, Thomas H. Louis, Zichao Zhang, and Yuh Min Chook, **Rules for Nuclear Localization Sequence Recognition by Karyopherinβ2**, Cell (2006) 126(3):543-558.

[Leung2003] Sara W. Leung, Michelle T. Harreman, Mary R. Hodel, Alec E. Hodel, Anita H. Corbett, **Dissection of the Karyopherin α Nuclear Localization Signal (NLS)-binding Groove: FUNCTIONAL REQUIREMENTS FOR NLS BINDING**, J. Biol.Chem(2003) 278: 41947-41953.

[Li2001] Weizhong Li, Lukasz Jaroszewski, Adam Godzik, **Clustering of highly homologous sequences to reduce the size of large protein database**, Bioinformatics, (2001) 17:282-283.

[Lin2013] Jhih-rong Lin, Jianjun Hu, **SeqNLS: Nuclear Localization Signal Prediction Based on Frequent Pattern Mining and Linear Motif Scoring**, PLOS ONE (2013).

[Marfori2011] Mary Marfori, Andrew Mynott, Jonathan J. Ellis, Ahmed M. Mehdi, Neil F.W. Saunders, Paul M. Curmi, Jade K. Forwood, Mikael Bodén, Bostjan Kobe, **Molecular basis for specificity of nuclear import and prediction of nuclear localization**, Biochimica et Biophysica Acta (2011) 1562–1577.

[Mika2003] Sven Mika, Burkhard Rost, **UniqueProt: creating representative protein sequence sets**, Nucleic Acids Research (2003) 31: 3789–3791.

[Nakai1999] Nakai K, Horton P, **PSORT: a program for detecting sorting signals in proteins and predicting their subcellular localization**, Trends Biochem Sci. (1999) 24(1):34-6.

[Nair2003] Rajesh Nair, Phil Carter, Burkhard Rost, **NLSdb: database of nuclear localization signals**, Nucleic Acids Research (2003) 31:397-399.

[Nair2005] Nair R, Rost B, **Mimicking cellular sorting improves prediction of subcellular localization**, J Mol Biol. (2005) 348(1):85-100.

[Rost1999] Rost B, **Twilight zone of protein sequence alignments**, Protein Eng. (1999) 12(2):85-94.

[Sander1991] Sander C, Schneider R.,**Database of homology-derived protein structures and the structural meaning of sequence alignment**, Proteins (1991)9(1):56-68.

[Santisteban2012] Iraia GARC´IA-SANTISTEBAN, Sonia BA ˜NUELOS, Jose A. RODR´IGUEZ, **A global survey of CRM1-dependent nuclear export sequences in the human deubiquitinase family**, Biochemie J. (2012) 441:209-217.

[Shimizu1998] Kazuya Shimizu, Hiromichi Shirataki, Tomoyuki Honda, Seigo Minami, Yoshimi Takai, **Complex Formation of SMAP/KAP3, a KIF3A/B ATPase Motor-associated Protein, with a Human Chromosome-associated Polypeptide**, THE JOURNAL OF BIOLOGICAL CHEMISTRY (1998) 273:6591–6594.

[Sievers2011]   Fabian Sievers, Andreas Wilm, David Dineen, Toby J Gibson, Kevin Karplus, Weizhong Li, Rodrigo Lopez, Hamish McWilliam, Michael Remmert, Johannes Söding, Julie D Thompson and Desmond G Higgins, **Fast, scalable generation of high-quality protein multiple sequence alignments using Clustal Omega**, Molecular Systems Biology (2011) 7: 539.

[Sigrist2010]   Sigrist CJ, Cerutti L, de Castro E, Langendijk-Genevaux PS, Bulliard V, Bairoch A, Hulo N, **PROSITE, a protein domain database for functional characterization and annotation**, Nucleic Acids Res. (2010) 38:161-166

[Sneath1973]   Sneath, Sokal, **Numerical Taxonomy**, Freeman (1973).

[Süel2008]   Katherine E. Süel, Hongmei Gu, Yuh Min Chook, **Modular Organization and Combinatorial Energetics of Proline–Tyrosine Nuclear Localization Signals**, PLoS Biology (2008).

[Pomeranz1999]   LISA E. POMERANZ, JOHN A. BLAHO, **Modified VP22 Localizes to the Cell Nucleus during Synchronized Herpes Simplex Virus Type 1 Infection**, Journal of Virology (1999) 73:6769-6781.

[PubMed]   http://www.ncbi.nlm.nih.gov/pubmed

[UniProt2015]   The UniProt Consortium, **UniProt: a hub for protein information**, Nucleic Acids Res. (2015) 43: D204-D212.

[UniProtID]   http://web.expasy.org/docs/userman.html#ID_line

[Verkman2002]   Alan S. Verkman, **Solute and macromolecule diffusion in cellular aqueous compartments**, TRENDS in Biochemical Sciences (2002) 1.

[Wagstaff2009]   Kylie M. Wagstaff, David A. Jans, **Importins and Beyond: Non-Conventional Nuclear Transport Mechanisms**, Traffic(2009) 10: 1188–1198.

[Wang2011]   Aiyuan Wang, Shengqiang Xu, Xiaoxian Zhang, Jie He, Donghui Yan, Zhangmin Yang and Sheng Xiao, **Ribosomal protein RPL41 induces rapid degradation of ATF4, a transcription factor critical for tumour cell survival in stress**, Journal of Pathology (2011) 225:285-292.

[Xu2012]   Darui Xu, Alicia Farmer, Garen Collett, Nick V. Grishin, Yuh Min Chook, **Sequence and structural analyses of nuclear export signals in the NESdb database**, Mol Biol Cell (2012) 18:3677-3693.

[Yachdav2014]   Yachdav G, Kloppmann E, Kajan L, Hecht M, Goldberg T, Hamp T, Hönigschmid P, Schafferhans A, Roos M, Bernhofer M, Richter L, Ashkenazy H, Punta M, Schlessinger A, Bromberg Y, Schneider R, Vriend G, Sander C, Ben-Tal N, Rost B, **PredictProtein--an open resource for online prediction of protein structural and functional features**, Nucleic Acids Research (2014) 42: 337–343.